Saffron Days in L.A.

Saffron Days in L.A.

TALES OF A BUDDHIST MONK IN AMERICA

Bhante Walpola Piyananda

FOREWORD BY THE DALAI LAMA

SHAMBHALA
Boston & London ■ 2001

Shambhala Publications, Inc.
Horticultural Hall
300 Massachusetts Avenue
Boston, Massachusetts 02115
www.shambhala.com

Printed in the United States of America

Distributed in the United States by Random House, Inc.,
and in Canada by Random House of Canada Ltd

Library of Congress Cataloging-in-Publication Data
Piyananda, Bhante Walpola.
Saffron days in L.A. : tales of a Buddhist monk in America /
Bhante Walpola Piyananda ; foreword by the Dalai Lama.
p.   cm.
Includes index.
ISBN 1-57062-813-0 (pbk.)
1. Religious life—Buddhism.   2. Buddhism—Doctrines.
I. Title: Tales of a Buddhist monk in America.   II. Title.
BQ 4302 .P59   2001
294.3'44—dc21
00-067962

BVG 01

I dedicate this book with reverence and gratitude to my parents and teachers who encouraged me to begin my spiritual journey.

CONTENTS

Foreword by the Dalai Lama   IX
Acknowledgments   XI
Introduction   XIII

ONE   The Robe   1

TWO   Phoenix Calamity   13

THREE   Religious Tolerance   21

FOUR   Boundless Compassion   28

FIVE   The Disciple Who Jumped
over the Cliff   34

SIX   The Punks Meet the Monk   42

SEVEN   The Balancing Act   54

EIGHT   Karmic Ties   60

NINE   Detachment—A Way of Life   73

TEN   A Lady of the Night   81

ELEVEN   Fidelity and Faith   93

TWELVE   Buddhist Prosperity   100

THIRTEEN   Healing Powers of Chanting   106

FOURTEEN   The London Doctor   115

FIFTEEN   Children Change Us   126

SIXTEEN   The Alcoholic   135

SEVENTEEN   Painful Consequences   143

EIGHTEEN   The Sunbather   149

NINETEEN   Appearances Are Deceiving   159

TWENTY   The Seven Types of Wealth   167

Glossary   177
Notes   179
About the Author   187

FOREWORD

Compassion is the key to Buddhism. If we can learn to act with compassion toward all living beings under all circumstances, then we will undoubtedly be happy ourselves. This book by Ven. Walpola Piyananda reveals such compassion directly, in stories that are based on his own experience.

Ven. Piyananda is a senior monk from Sri Lanka who has lived in the United States for more than twenty-three years. Here he has written a book that embodies well the approach of Theravada Buddhism, with lessons that are applicable to all schools of Buddhism. He has managed to relate his own extensive experience of dealing with people living in the United States, whether they are Asian or American, Buddhist or non-Buddhist, and set it all in the context of the Lord Buddha's teaching. In so doing, I believe he has created a book to which all readers can relate.

These stories are about what happens to us in everyday life. They provide vivid examples of how we can react most compassionately to what happens to us. Ven. Piyananda is well read in the Buddhist scriptures and is regularly able to cite what the Buddha had to say about this or that situation. Each of the stories told here relates to an event and how Ven. Piyananda was involved in it.

Ven. Piyananda possesses the admirable quality of never having compromised his identity as a traditionally trained Sri Lankan Theravadan Buddhist monk, and yet he always acts compassionately toward others, without wishing to impose his specific beliefs on the people with whom he comes in contact. Indeed, he makes the Buddha's teachings available whenever and wherever he goes, but with the simple and compassionate goal of helping people face up to whatever situations present themselves.

I believe that readers will find much to learn from in this book. But besides that, there are many incidents in it that are likely to raise a smile, which means that they will also enjoy it.

—*Tenzin Gyatso*
The Fourteenth Dalai Lama

ACKNOWLEDGMENTS

I would like to thank all the people in this book who enriched my experiences. Many stories and anecdotes are included in these chapters. Situations and events are true but to protect the privacy and confidentiality of those I've written about, I have changed some names and anecdotal details to prevent identifying any particular individual or situation. My goal is to teach the message of the Buddha as it is applied to our daily living.

First and foremost, I humbly thank all my teachers, especially Ven. Walpola Gnanaratana Maha Thera, who ordained me as a Buddhist monk.

I am grateful to His Holiness the Dalai Lama who wrote the foreword to my book amidst his busy schedule.

I thank Mr. Ron Bogan, who sponsored my coming to America, the late Ven. Neluwe Jinaratana Maha Nayaka Thera of India, Ven. Dr. K. Sri Dhammananda Maha Nayaka Thera of Malaysia, the late Ven. Dr. Walpola Rahula Maha Thera, Ven. Haupe Somananda Nayaka Maha Thera, and Dr. Ananda Guruge, who encouraged me to come to this great country.

I am grateful to the late Ven Dr. Havanpola Ratanasara Nayaka Maha Thera; Gamini Jayasinghe, M.D.; S. K. P. Gunawardane, M.D.; and the other members of the Dharma Vijaya Buddhist Vihara who thought righteously and supported me during my difficult early days in this country, as well as through other challenges I had to face over the years.

I would like to thank my colleague and *dhamma* brother Ven. Dr. Pannila Ananda Nayake Maha Thera, who has been beside me since childhood. I am also appreciative of the friendship and generosity of Ven. Madawala Seelawimala, my spiritual brother. My gratitude also to my teachers: the late Dr. Edmund Perry, Chairman, Department of Religion, Northwestern University; Dr. George Bond, formerly the Head of the Deparment of Religious Studies at Northwestern University; Dr. S. Scott Bartchy, Professor of Christian Origins and the History of Religion and Director of the Center for the Study of Religion at UCLA; and Dr. Chandra Wickramagamage, Senior Professor of Pali and Buddhist Studies at Jayawardhanapura University in Sri Lanka.

My special thanks to Bodhicari Sama (Dede Whiteside), Bodhicari Sanghamitta (Ramya Gunasekera), and Dhammacari Dharmapala (Stephen Long). I appreciate their patient, cheerful, tireless efforts, their insight and devotion in editing this book.

I thank Bodhicari Dharmajiva (Stan Levinson) for discussing some of the stories included in this book and for contributing to the copyediting.

I am thankful to the Ven. Weihene Pannaloka Nayaka Maha Thera, Ven. Dr. Udagama Sumangala Maha Thera, Ven. Madawala Punnaji Maha Thera, Ven. Koppakande Sumanajothi Thera, Ven. Siyabalagoda Ananda Thera, Ven. Watogala Saranasiri Thera, Cynthia Shimazu, Dhammika Vidanapathirana, Loku Banda Tillakaratne, Ramani Priyanka, Vasana De Mel, Anura Jayatilake, Gananath Wijeratne, Tissa Karunasiri, Ana Scott Kadin, Bhadraji Jayatileka, Dr. Bandula Wijay, Shani Wijay, Duminda Gamage, Amali Jayasinghe, and Purnika Liyanage for their valuable assistance.

Finally, I wish to thank Shambhala Publications for publishing this book.

May they all enjoy the blessings of the Triple Gem. May they all be well and happy.

W. P.

INTRODUCTION

It is almost twenty-five years since I came to this country, and I have encountered many experiences I never even imagined while growing up in Sri Lanka. I believe I have brought some unique experiences to those who have come in contact with me.

After completing my postgraduate studies in India, I went back to my native Sri Lanka to give service as a monk, but I had a strong urge to go to America. My superiors and colleagues tried to dissuade me. They warned me, based on information they had mostly only heard. They believed America was a dangerous place for someone dressed as a Buddhist monk and that it was not ready for the teachings of the Buddha. Also, they said, the temptations were so great that I might wind up giving up my robes and living a secular, materialistic life.

But I had great faith in the Buddha, in the Dhamma, and in the Sangha, and I was confident that my training would enable me to disseminate the Buddha's teachings in America. I recalled the Punnovada Sutta. Punna was a monk who was determined to move to another country. The Buddha warned him, but his warning was a kind of test of Ven. Punna.

"Punna, the people of Sunaparanta are fierce and rough. If they abuse and threaten you, what will you think then?"

"Venerable Sir, I'll think "These people of Sunaparanta are excellent, truly excellent, in that they did not give me a blow with the fist.""

"And if they hit you?"

"Then I'll think that they did not give me a blow with a clod."

"And if they hit you with a clod?"

"That they did not give me a blow with a stick."

"And if they hit you with a stick?"

"That they did not stab me with a knife."

"And if they stab you with a knife?"

"That they did not take my life with the knife."

"And if they take your life with the knife?"

"There have been disciples of the Blessed One, who, being repelled, humiliated, and disgusted by the body and by life, have sought an assailant. But I have obtained an assailant without even a search."

The Buddha replied, "Good, good, Punna! Possessing such self-control and peacefulness, you will be able to dwell in the Sunaparanta country."

The story of Punna had left an indelible message in my mind. Therefore, I decided amidst all obstacles to pursue my desire to venture into the "New World."

No one has stabbed me, hit me with a stick, a clod, or a hand, or even tried to kill me, though I've had some pretty exciting adventures. In this book I try to show how in each experience, whether sad, happy, funny, serious, or even tragic, there is a lesson to be learned. It is because of the Buddha's teachings that I have been able to handle and learn from these situations and, hopefully, help others.

In fact, I am happy to mention that while being a traditional saffron-robed monk, I am able to live a fruitful life being of service to humanity in this great land of freedom, equality, and opportunity.

I hope you will find the following stories entertaining and beneficial. May you be well and happy.

Saffron Days in L.A.

ONE

The Robe

It had been two months since I ordained Sunanda. It is not an easy adjustment to become a Buddhist monk. It was especially difficult for Sunanda, who was not only a Westerner, but was born and raised in the Jewish faith in Beverly Hills. He had not been brought up around monks, or in a culture that knew about, incorporated, and honored the *sangha* as an essential part of society, as it is in most of Asia.

Sunanda had been struggling quietly with a few issues, and he thought I had not noticed. I decided to wait for him to come forward to ask for help, knowing that he needed to choose his own time. As the waters of his frustration rose, the dam holding his silence eventually broke on a clear early sunrise in the spring.

Sunanda usually came to my room in the morning to pay his respects to me as his teacher and abbot, a tradition he seemed to enjoy and appreciate. Even though he was always friendly, he was often quiet and usually spent only a few moments with me, eager to begin his daily work. On this particular spring day his face was full of concern and question, and he stayed with me longer than usual.

He suddenly shouted out loud, "Bhante!" The force of his voice, coming from such a usually quiet monk, sent a shock wave through the room. I turned and looked at him with amazement.

"Bhante!" he called out again. "I think I have to give up my robe. I have to leave the monastery!"

Sunanda's eyes were downcast, and I could tell that he was having a difficult time getting up the courage to face me. I knew that this was the time to talk at last. "Sunanda," I calmly said, "please tell me what's on your mind. You are obviously troubled. Perhaps I can be of assistance to you."

He looked at me with trepidation, like he wished he had not spoken out so abruptly. "It's OK," I said. "Please feel free to continue. That's how we learn. There is nothing you could say to me that would shock me."

Sunanda looked at me again for reassurance, and I nodded. He took a deep breath and began.

"Bhante, I am so embarrassed about what I am going to tell you. Since I was ordained a couple of months ago, I have been harassed endlessly. People yell out names, whisper as I pass, ask me if I forgot to change my Halloween costume! They say, 'Hey, are you a pumpkin?' They have kicked me on the bus. Sometimes I think I will be beaten up! I am afraid to go outside. How can I live this way, Bhante? I don't know what to do."

Sunanda was starting to sob, thinking about the abuse he had endured. I am sure he was also thinking about the possibility of giving up his vows. He was a devoted Buddhist monk, and I could well understand the pain he was feeling.

"My dear Sunanda," I said, in a reassuring manner. "You are not alone. I have suffered the same treatment on many occasions."

Sunanda looked up at me, absolutely startled. "You *what*?" he said with widening eyes. "How could anyone abuse someone like you?"

"Well, I will tell you, Sunanda. I'll share a few stories with you and then you'll understand."

Sunanda nodded and then moved closer so he could hear me better. He obviously didn't want to miss a word of what I was about to say.

"Sunanda, a few months ago I was traveling with Bhante Sumedha and Nanda from Los Angeles to Berkeley. Do you remember that trip?"

Sunanda nodded his head and I continued.

"We stopped at a rest area to go to the bathroom. As I was going into the men's room, a man stopped me and shouted, 'Hey, this isn't the women's bathroom!' I ignored him. Then again he called out, 'Hey, lady! Don't you understand English? This isn't the women's bathroom!'

"I removed the knit cap on my head and turned to face the man. 'Sir, I am a Buddhist monk. I am wearing a traditional monk's robe.'

"The man was completely taken aback and he replied, 'Oh, I am sorry, sir. I thought you were wearing an Indian sari!'

"When I walked back outside, the man was standing there waiting for me. He approached, and with excitement in his voice, he asked if he could speak with me. I quietly nodded my head in consent."

"Bhante, please continue," Sunanda urged, filled with curiosity.

I leaned forward and spoke with more vigor. "He wanted to know my name. I told him that I am called Bhante.

"'Bhante, my name is Bill,' he replied. 'I am so curious about your dress. Or rather your robe! Please tell me about its colors. Bright yellow. Hmm. What does that mean?' Bill questioned.

"I replied, 'Yellow is a cheerful, lovely color. Yellow is associated with happiness and is known as the color of the intellect; therefore, yellow represents a sense of mindfulness. The color yellow symbolizes maturity—a ripe mango has a saffron hue. Yellow is also the color of the rising sun, which shines equally on everything on this planet. It does not discriminate when it brightens the world. In the same manner, a monk who wears a yellow robe should treat all equally.[1] I'm neither a follower of self-mortification, nor do I lead an indulgent life.[2] I follow a path called the Middle Path, which is represented by yellow, one of the three primary colors, located on the spectrum between red and blue."

"What do you mean 'Middle Path'?" asked Bill, genuinely wanting to know.

"Well, the Middle Path avoids extremes. One is the way of extreme indulgence in or attachment to sense pleasures. In this way one looks for happiness through the gratification of the senses. In the other way, the way of self-mortification, one rejects the senses. One way depends on attachment to the senses, while the other way denies them. Yellow is in between, presenting the idea of the Middle Path. A person who practices the Middle Path can gain vision and knowledge, which leads to a tranquil, balanced personality.

"Bill thanked me. His wife was signaling him to return to their RV, which was parked under a tree on the other side of the rest area. We parted company with a smile."

Sunanda had been listening to my story in amazement. Again he urged me to tell him more.

"In 1977, while at Northwestern University, I went on the El and got off at State Street. I was waiting for a bus that would take me to the Thai Buddhist Temple. Two young women and three young men came up to me, threatened me with foul language, and forced me to go with them. They kept calling me a Hari Krishna. They even accused me of being involved with some recent news headlines regarding the Hari Krishnas, one of which involved the kidnapping of a girl. They said they were going to kill me. Finally I got them to calm down somewhat, and I showed them my Northwestern ID card. They looked back and forth at one another, completely baffled, and I explained that I was a Buddhist monk.

"One girl asked, 'Then why do you wear Hari Krishna clothes?'

"I explained to them that it was a traditional Buddhist monk's robe. Eventually they apologized, saying they were convinced I was not a Hari Krishna. I told them that Hari Krishnas always have a ponytail, and I do not have a ponytail. I showed them my clean-shaven head. They finally got the message and let me go.

"Another incident occurred about a year after my arrival in Los Angeles. This time a Thai family had invited me for *dana* at their apartment in the Mid-Wilshire district. Kamal, a layman residing in the temple, drove me there. We got to the lobby of the apartment complex about forty-five minutes early. So, while Kamal went looking for a place to park the car, I waited for him in the lobby, where a woman was seated on a couch in the corner.

"As I waited, I decided to make sure that my robe was worn according to Theravada customs. Donning the robe is a reflection of the philosophy of *dhamma,* and an art in itself. Every crease and every fold has a meaning and a purpose. Carefully, I rolled one corner of the outer fold of the cloth and shaped it into a robe. While doing so, I spread the other fold of the cloth over my head, which completely covered my face. Then I wrapped the rolled fold of the robe around my neck before bringing the fold covering my head and face down over my shoulders. While my face was still covered, I saw the shadow of the woman on the couch rush past me to the elevator.

"No sooner had I finished arranging my robe than I heard the fire sirens approaching around the corner. Within seconds, police cruisers and an ambulance pulled up in front of the lobby. The policemen and paramedics came running, and as they approached I could see looks of utter astonishment on their faces. One officer stepped forward and asked me brusquely what I was trying to do. I was totally confused by then, and I asked the group of would-be rescuers if someone would please explain what was going on.

"The first police officer said, 'A woman called nine-one-one and reported an attempted suicide in the lobby. She told the dispatcher that an Indian guru was trying to suffocate himself with his long dress!'

"By now Kamal was just coming into the lobby. He, too, asked what was happening. Quickly, an officer took him aside and began questioning him.

"After realizing the mistake made by the caller, I explained to the officers what must have happened. I demonstrated the folding of the robe to the delight of the officers and paramedics. They promptly apologized for the inconvenience the whole episode had caused.

"When the news that the police were questioning a monk in the lobby filtered up to the seventh-story apartment of my Thai hosts, they came running down to save me. We all enjoyed a good laugh over that one."

Sunanda couldn't help but laugh, and I could feel his mood lightening.

I continued. "Another time I had to go to Minneapolis for religious services. I went to O'Hare Airport to catch the plane. I didn't know what gate to go to or how to find out. I asked many people, but everyone looked at me with disdain. Not one person responded to my pleas for information. Even the woman at one of the counters told me, 'Go away! You are not supposed to be here.'

"Then I ran up to a police officer. Before I asked him

where to go, he said, 'If you don't leave this airport, I will arrest you! Get out of here right now!'

"I shouted back at him, 'I don't want to go to jail, officer. I want to go to Minneapolis!' Then I showed the officer my boarding pass. He blushed and very sheepishly told me where the gate was. Relieved, I ran off, wondering why all the people were being so unfriendly toward me."

"Oh Bhante, you are so brave," exclaimed Sunanda at this point. "They, too, must have thought you were a Hari Krishna."

"Not an uncommon mistake," I replied, watching Sunanda's reaction.

I continued. "Let me tell you another story. Once, in 1976, I was standing at a bus stop at the corner of Vine Street and Hollywood Boulevard. I was on my way to the bookstore. A couple of other people were also waiting at the bus stop. Suddenly, a gentleman in a Mercedes Benz stopped at the curb, ran up to me, and spit in my face. He screamed at me, 'You do not belong in this country. Go away!'

"Then I responded politely, 'Thank you so much for your advice.'

"The other people were both sad and angry. One lady reached into her purse and gave me a tissue so I could wipe off my face. She said, 'Don't worry, sir. He must be some kind of crazy fundamentalist. Not all Americans are like that.'

"I said I understood. Then she expressed her opinion that if I could travel in regular clothes, not in my monk's robes, people probably wouldn't harass me. I responded, 'No, I am a Buddhist monk. I choose to wear these robes to teach people about the Buddha.'"

Sunanda said, "I heard that Theravada senior monks in Europe and on the East Coast wear coats over their robes."

"It could be because of the climate," I replied. "I've never heard of a senior monk wearing one because of prejudice against him. They wear coats over their robes when they go outside the temple in cold weather."

"Why don't we introduce this attire here?" he asked.

I told Sunanda that the Buddha designed this robe because it has great symbolic meaning.

"What is that?" asked Sunanda. "Why did the Buddha ask us to wear this robe?"

"As monks, we have to understand completely the teaching about impermanence. In autumn, the leaves are yellow and orange. Do these leaves belong to the tree or to the ground, Sunanda?"

"Bhante, they don't belong to either. While they are on the tree, they belong to the tree, but at any moment they may fall to the ground and belong to the ground."

"That's right, Sunanda. We must understand that everything is subject to change, even as we are. As Bhante Gunaratana says, even as I am talking to you, every molecule and particle in our bodies is constantly changing. The neurons in our brains die, and millions of our blood cells die every moment without our realizing it.[3] Change is continuously taking place without our even being aware that it is happening. Can we relive our most pleasant feelings exactly as we experienced them the first time? Can we recreate those exact situations and enjoy those same feelings again? No, my friend, we cannot. Similarly, the feelings you are experiencing now may change at any moment. They may even turn to disappointment or to pain."

"Does this apply to human relationships also, Bhante?"

"Yes, people find that they make mistakes in their associations because they fail to be aware that both parties are constantly changing. One must realize that people and situations are impermanent."

"Oh yes, Bhante, I recall how disappointed my parents were when I became a monk. They even disinherited me.

However, today they are pleased with my decision, and even consult me on important issues. Now they have appointed me as a trustee of my father's estate."

"I am glad you have come to understand the impermanence of life and feelings, Sunanda. A person who wears this robe is an embodiment of peace, harmony, and universal love."

"Why did the Buddha design this robe?" he asked again.

"In ancient times, monks wore a single piece of whatever cloth they could find. Some wore one color; others wore another color. Once, a group of monks went to bathe at the Ganges River. Upon returning to the riverbank they noticed that their robes had been stolen. Then they went to the Buddha to complain. The Buddha used that incident as the opportunity to design new robes for the protection of the monks, as well as to give them their symbolic meaning.

"The Buddha contemplated the rice paddy fields that covered the land. He said to his disciple Ananda, 'Do you see how the land of Magadha is laid out in squares, strips, borders, and cross lines?'

"'Yes, Lord,' replied the faithful disciple.

"'Then try to arrange robes like that for the monks, Ananda.'[4]

"The Buddha thought that good monks were like good farmers. Therefore, the robes should be modeled after a paddy field. The paddy field is made up of irrigated segments, an excellent arrangement for developing a good field. Monks cultivate a field of wholesomeness for themselves, as well as for the community in which they live.

"A good farmer protects the paddy field, not allowing cows, pigs, elephants, birds, or wild animals to destroy the field. He prevents the destruction of the field in every way he can. Similarly, monks have to prevent the misuse of their five senses, which helps them to protect themselves from being destroyed.

"As a good farmer removes weeds, rocks, and any materials harmful to his field, likewise a monk removes any defilement, such as anger, hate, ill will, and jealousy, from his mind. When a thought comes to his mind that produces defilement, he removes that anger or ill will and his mind becomes pure again, just as a field becomes ready for cultivation once weeds and rocks have been removed.

"In the same way as a farmer cultivates his field with the best rice seed and plants in the right season at the right time—first fertilizing the soil and making sure the seeds have the best conditions for growth—so monks must cultivate good deeds like love, compassion, sympathetic joy, and equanimity.

"So you see, Sunanda, the robe has an important meaning that we must keep in mind, and by wearing it, we can use it as a tool to teach those around us."

I could tell that Sunanda had understood what I was trying to share with him.

I kept a close eye on Sunanda for the next few weeks. I sensed that he was more serene and collected in his behavior. I gave him a copy of a poem written by one of my students, Sama Dede Whiteside. I would like to share it with you here.

> The Robe
> Ochre and Citron
> Yellow and Orange
> Flowing Movement Told
> Of Sacred Robe's Presage
> Divine Symbol's Folds
>
> Farmer of Five
> Fields of Festivity
> Sown Together
> Sow,

Fisher of Men
Dhamma Teacher
Farmer
Of Fields
Of Inquiry
Your Tools—
Seeds, Weeds, Wind, Water

Dhamma, Hindrances,
    Lovingkindness
Sun's Soft Touch
Morning's Warm Caresses
Breathing Dew
From Her Children's Coats
Precipitating Liquids
Returned as Fire

Seeds, Weeds, Wind, Water
Dhamma, Hindrances, Lovingkindness
Generate, Remove, Harvest
Crop of Freedom Shared
With and For Each Hearing Heart

Rice Fields' Irrigation
Lifted Beyond
Horizons Bounds
Propelling
Force of Water-Wind

Sequence Overflow
Gating into Transformations
Moving Channels
Opening
Changing
Ever Changing River

> Without Bounds?
> Within Boundlessness?
> Boundlessness of Neither
> Within or Without
> Endless Seas of No Dimension
> Love

I am glad to say that Sunanda is now a very learned monk who regularly practices meditation and serves the community with all his heart.

> Whoever is master of his own Nature,
> Bright, clear and true,
> He may indeed wear the yellow robe.[5]

TWO

Phoenix Calamity

When I arrived in America on July 4, 1976, I knew hardly anyone. I had made arrangements to land in San Francisco and stay for one week at the Gold Mountain Chinese Monastery. I will never forget my arrival day. When the monks from the monastery picked me up at the airport they took me directly to the big Bicentennial Parade, which was just about to begin. The monastery had entered a "float" in the parade, on top of which rode a large Buddha statue. Without hesitation, the monks ushered me right up onto the top of the float and told me to sit next to the Buddha statue and hold its arm to help steady it. I tell you, riding through the streets of San Francisco on a Buddhist float on the two-hundredth anniversary of America was quite a moment for me indeed!

After my week in San Francisco I went down to Los Angeles and lived for a while at the International Buddhist Meditation Center. The abbot and founder of the center was Thich Thien-An, one of the first Vietnamese monks in America. He established many temples in the United States and was the founder of the United Buddhist Churches in America. He was a wise and compassionate monk who helped many refugees. Thich Thien-An was a member of the Mahayana Buddhist order. On the West Coast most people had never heard of Theravada monks.

One Saturday afternoon in July, I decided to take a walk. Since the IBMC was located in one of the most diverse neighborhoods in Los Angeles, I had the intuition that I would meet someone who would be interested in Buddhism.

I had hardly walked two blocks from the center when I saw a little woman approach me expressing a great deal of joy. As I neared her, I noticed that she appeared to be a woman of Asian origin. She was pushing a child in a stroller.

She reached me and kneeled down and bowed before me in the customary manner of Southeast Asian countries. She smiled broadly and told me how happy she was to see a Buddhist monk. She told me that her name was Soondaree, and she said she was from Thailand. We talked for a few moments, and then she got very excited and said, "*Ajarn* (teacher), you must come to my house for *Bindabata* tomorrow morning. I will make food for you!" *Bindabata* is the Thai translation of the Pali term *pindopatha,* meaning the receiving of alms.

Having spent a great deal of time in Thailand, I knew that every morning all Buddhist monks go with their bowls to receive alms. Even the king, during the period when he himself was a monk at the age of twenty, was not exempted from this rule. No matter where you go in Thailand, you can never forget the image of waking up early in the morning and going out into the city streets or country villages and seeing the solitary, barefooted monks silently passing from door to door, holding out their bowls to the people who stand to the side bowing and reverently offering food. The

Buddha advised the monks to go seeking alms to help eradicate their egos. Giving alms to monks also helps the society gain merit.[1]

The minute Soondaree invited me for alms, I realized that I had not brought an alms bowl from Sri Lanka, as in my home country, this practice is slowly diminishing.

I was in a quandary. I knew I had to make Soondaree happy, because the Buddha taught us that we should always try to make others happy. If an individual believes in us, the Buddha wanted us to manifest this faith for that individual.

I knew I had to somehow find a bowl. I spoke to my friend Kirk and asked him where I could buy an alms bowl. He laughed and told me to carry a clay flowerpot!

I laughed at the notion, too, but Kirk wound up taking me to a nursery nearby, and we bought a round clay pot. The trouble was, it was brown, and I needed the requisite black bowl!

Kirk, still laughing, came to my rescue. He bought a can of spray paint and sprayed the bowl black. Now I was ready for my visit.

The next day, as promised, I went to Soondaree's house to formally receive alms from her household. As I stood in front of their doorstep, Soondaree and her family, in the traditional way, offered me alms. Their friends from Thailand were also lined up along the path to offer me alms as well. I was quite surprised to see the turnout.

As I stood on the sidewalk, my head humbly bowed, my bowl began to overflow with various kinds of offerings including food, medicine, flowers, and incense. Some of the people also discreetly offered me cash in sealed white envelopes.

In the meantime, this scene began to attract a small crowd of inquisitive observers from the surrounding neighborhood, which was an ethnic mix of Latinos, Caucasians, and other Asians.

I heard the Thais explaining to the non-Buddhists this Buddhist practice of giving alms. Those who had never seen it were very curious. When I was ready to leave, Soondaree asked me to please visit every day; the Thais in the neighborhood wanted to have the opportunity to offer a Buddhist monk alms, as they would do in their native country.

I granted their request and, without fail, made my alms rounds every morning. A Chinese monk, Dhammajothi, later joined me on this daily routine.

The community was happy; therefore, I was happy. The news of my activity spread very rapidly and one of my teachers, the Ven. Dr. Walpola Rahula, called me on the telephone from London. He discouraged me from alms collecting because most Westerners were not familiar with the practices of ancient Buddhist traditions. He was of the opinion that alms collection would give the incorrect impression to American society that monks are all beggars.[2]

I easily understood why he was concerned, knowing that Buddhist monks had the obligation to avoid giving the wrong signals to their host societies wherever they were. Much to the disappointment of my new Thai devotees, I immediately gave up my practice of *pindapatha*.

The Thai people continued to seek my spiritual advice, however, and they kindly looked after me and made sure I had everything I needed. I continue this relationship with my many Thai friends even to this day. I am with them on happy occasions as well as in their times of sorrow.

One day in August 1991, I was shocked to hear about the massacre at the Thai temple in Phoenix, Arizona. Six monks, one novice, one nun, and a lay devotee had been brutally shot to death in the Shrine Room.

I flew to Phoenix immediately, accompanied by Nampet, a Thai activist and community spokesperson. She was devastated and deeply saddened by the cold-blooded violence against the monks. She said to me, "Bhante, it is extremely difficult for me to not feel negative toward those murderers who committed this crime. Even though I practice meditation every day, and my Buddhist name is Metta, which means loving kindness, I find it so hard to extend my *metta* toward those responsible."

"Nampet, what you are feeling is natural during this early stage of shock. I am sure that with a little time you will be able to ease your strong feelings. This reminds me of the time I was with the Dalai Lama in 1978, and he was asked the question, 'If you were to meet Mao Tse-tung today, what would you do?' The Dalai Lama smiled and answered politely, 'Mao Tse-tung is my teacher and I respect him.' We were all taken completely by surprise at the Dalai Lama's response, given what the Chinese had done to him and his people.

"The Dalai Lama said, 'It is true that Mao Tse-tung destroyed my monasteries, killed many of my people including innocent monks, took away my country and my home, and caused me to become a refugee along with thousands of other Tibetans. On the other hand, since I was four years old I was sheltered and protected and taught meditation and spiritual doctrine, including the daily blessing of all living things—even my enemies. But you see, I never had any object to focus my loving kindness on since I had no obstacles. With Mao Tse-tung I had an object, one whom I could forgive and love in spite of what he had done to me and my people.'

"So, Nampet, please think of the Dalai Lama's words of compassion, and try your best to forgive these murderers."

This was a difficult task, in light of the tremendous shock and grief that Nampet and all of us had suffered. Eventually, however, she was able to deal with her feelings of frustration.

We arrived at the temple in Phoenix, which, by then, was packed with grieving monks and emotionally distraught devotees. The FBI, television crews, other news media, and state officials were also there in great numbers.

I talked to many people at the scene and soon became overwhelmed by some of the wild rumors that were circulating. Many were saying that the murders had been a hate crime. Some were saying that it was a robbery. Others were claiming that it was some sort of gang retaliation. All of these speculations added to the general confusion and state of upset.

Some Buddhists were of the opinion that it was an attack to stop the spread of Asian religions. Some believed that extremist groups either did it or inspired it.

After discussing the situation with the other monks who had flown in to help with damage control, I decided that my first priority would be to console the mourners.

At the funeral service I was selected to deliver the eulogy. This gave me the opportunity to express my views as follows:

America is the land of freedom, equality, and opportunity. This is the country of great blessings for everybody. Two days ago seven Buddhist monks, one nun, and a lay devotee left us unexpectedly, without enjoying this freedom, equality, and liberty. It may seem difficult to recall the tragedy without a stirring of our emotions. We gather here not to think of revenge or to give vent to our anger, but to practice compassion, forgiveness, and reconciliation.

This incident was caused by greed, hatred, anger, ignorance, and delusion. Many leaders like Abraham Lincoln, Mahatma Gandhi, the Kennedys, and Martin Luther King, Jr. fell victim to assassins who were beset by these evils.

We as Buddhists have the weapons to fight these evil forces. Do not forget that the Lord Buddha armed us with excellent weapons: *metta* (love), *karuna* (compassion), *mudita* (appreciative joy), and *upekkha* (equanimity).[3]

> We fight anger with loving kindness.
> We fight cruelty with compassion.
> We fight jealousy with appreciative joy.
> We fight desire with equanimity.
> We fight ignorance with wisdom.

Our Lord Buddha taught us, "Hate is never overcome by hate. By love is hatred overcome. This is the eternal law."

Dear friends, as you know, the Buddhist monks in their yellow robes are the epitome of nonviolence. To Asians, yellow means peace, calm, and innocence. As Buddhist monks, we own no wealth. We do not crave power. We harm no one. We are trained not to kill even insects. We mind no one else's business. We renounce our ties to worldly affairs. Therefore, this incident is the result of the hatred, anger, and ill will festering in the minds of a few individuals due to their ignorance.

Let us aim at creating a society where calm and peace prevail over conquest and defeat; where the persecution of the innocent is vigorously denounced; where one who conquers oneself is more respected than those who conquer millions by military might; where hatred is conquered by love.

Let compassion be the driving force of our action; let all living beings be treated with fairness; and let peace and harmony reign in our hearts.

We must drop all our negative feelings, dedicate ourselves to good thought and good actions, and have faith in the ability of each individual to overcome hatred through love.

May all, including those who committed this crime, and the seven monks, the nun, and the lay devotee who fell victim to the crime, and all living beings, realize the ultimate truth, *nibbana*.

> May the suffering be free from suffering,
> The ill free from illness,
> The grieving free from grief.
> May all be well and happy.

My speech was published in the *Arizona Tribune* under the headline, "Monk Preaches Forgiveness at Ceremony." It was also published in the Buddhist magazine *TriCycle*. The whole calamity in Phoenix was a true test for all members of the *sangha*, as well as for Buddhists everywhere. We were all given the chance to put to practice our beliefs about living the life of sharing loving kindness with all beings, and sharing it unconditionally.

> Hatred never ceases through hatred
>   in this world.
> By non-hatred alone does hatred cease.
> This is a Law Eternal.[4]

THREE

Religious Tolerance

When I went to Northwestern University in 1976, I was the only Sri Lankan on campus. At times I felt homesick, especially during the winter months. Often I would dream of my tropical motherland.

One day when I was reading a Chicago newspaper, I saw an item announcing that the Sri Lankan ambassador was going to present an elephant to the Chicago zoo. I got very excited and spoke to my friend and professor, Dr. George Bond, about it. He offered to take me to the function, and we got there just before it started.

I saw three chairs and three gentlemen seated on the chairs. The large assembly of people was standing, since there were no other chairs. We mingled with the crowd for a while, and then a police officer informed me that I was wanted on the stage, so I followed him. Our Sri Lankan ambassador gave me his seat, and the governor of Illinois gave his seat to the ambassador. Immediately afterward another chair was brought on stage. The ambassador, Dr. Neville Kanakaratne, whispered to the mayor of Chicago that in Sri

Lanka Buddhist monks are always respected and given a place of honor.

The ambassador bowed and asked me to chant *pirith* (blessings). When I went to the podium, Dr. Kanakaratna got up and was followed by the governor and the mayor. Local Chicago television stations covered the event, and I will never forget the way our ambassador talked about the elephant he was presenting, using it as a metaphor to explain to the audience the Eightfold Path as taught by the Buddha. After the ceremony I returned home with a light heart because I had met a few fellow Sri Lankans.

Later that same day, while I was relaxing in my room, the telephone rang. To my great surprise, it was from Gauri Gupta, a daughter of one of my professors at Calcutta University. She had seen the midday news on television and spotted me chanting *pirith* during the ceremony. She was so happy to see me that she called the Sri Lankan embassy in Washington, D.C., and one of the consular officials gave her my telephone number.

Three years before, when I was living in Calcutta, I associated very closely with Dr. Gupta, my professor, and his family. I recalled attending Gauri's wedding to Dr. Desai, who was from Kerala.

As soon as she heard my voice on the telephone, Gauri immediately began telling me her problems. I knew that she felt isolated in Chicago, and I could tell that she was happy to have me as her confidant. Gauri's chief complaint was that her life was hell due to religious differences within her family. Dr. Desai, her husband, was born a Catholic, and he was a staunch believer in his faith. He had insisted that Gauri convert to Catholicism and that they raise their children as Catholics. Gauri could accept bringing up the children in the Catholic church, but disliked being forced to follow her husband's religious practices herself.

Gauri started to cry, saying, "My husband promised

before marriage not to interfere with my faith. My father is a faithful follower of Buddhism. I was brought up as a Buddhist. How can I go to church and follow their rituals? I don't believe in them, so I embarrass him by not respecting the priest. When the priest tells the congregation to kneel, I remain seated. This annoys my husband tremendously, so when we return home we inevitably have an argument. Bhante, I would like to return to my parents in India."

I responded, "I would like to talk to Dr. Desai. Please tell him to call me when he comes home from work. In the meantime, let's you and I talk about your situation. Gauri, I know how difficult it is for you to handle this. However, you must not ruin your relationship with your husband over your religious beliefs. All religions guide us to lead good lives. So please be patient and refrain from arguments with your husband."

I could tell that Gauri wasn't pleased to hear my advice, but she said obediently, "I'll try."

The following day I was surprised to see Dr. Desai and his family on my doorstep. I welcomed them warmly and thanked them for the fruits and the sweets they had brought. Dr. Desai was delighted to hear that I was studying Christianity at Northwestern University. At the same time, he was wondering why I was living in a Methodist seminary. I told him that Northwestern was affiliated with the Methodist church, but that I was also interested in Catholicism. I explained to him that at that time I was writing a paper on Catholic rites and rituals, comparing them to Buddhism. I conveyed to him my desire to visit a Catholic church, so he offered to take me with him the following Sunday.

As promised, Dr. Desai picked me up at my dormitory and took me to church with his family. I sat with them in a front pew. I was determined to show Gauri that I respected all religions; therefore, I did as the Romans did and followed along with the Catholic rituals. Gauri watched as I kneeled with the others while she stayed stubbornly seated. I looked over at her and caught her staring at me in amazement. After the service, Dr. Desai invited me home to have lunch with the family.

As we drove to his home, Dr. Desai started the conversation, "Bhante, I very much respect your open, tolerant outlook. Our pastor remarked to me about your respectful manner during the service. Gauri, did you see how Bhante conducted himself? He is a Buddhist monk, wearing a robe, but still he respected the words of the priest during the service. He is not a follower of Christ, yet he knows how to conduct himself in every situation. Bhante, what do you have to say about Gauri's behavior and attitude?"

I replied, "Dr. Desai, Gauri has not been exposed to other religions. She is used to Buddhist rituals. You have made going to church mandatory, and she detests it. She may be thinking you are trying to convert her, because as you may remember, in the olden days Christian missionaries forcefully converted people with a Bible and a sword. This happened not only in India, but also in Sri Lanka. However, the Buddha did not criticize or condemn any religion; in fact, he sought to enlighten people by showing them not to go to extremes. The Buddha did not say that Buddhism is the only true religion in the world, but rather exhorted people to accept and respect truth wherever it was found. The Buddha wanted to point out only one thing, and that is Truth. As you know, all of his teachings are based on the Four Noble Truths.

"I am sure that you would have heard about Emperor Asoka, who ruled India in the third century BCE. He was a highly enthusiastic follower of Buddhism who did his best to spread the doctrine throughout the world. Even Asoka, on his famous rock edict XII, inscribed in stone that one should respect all religions. This is written on a pillar at Karnataka in Santi, not far from your home. The next time you go back to India, you must visit this village and read the edict yourself."

"Bhante, did Emperor Asoka really say this?" asked Gauri.

"Yes, Gauri, in fact I remember the words:

> One should not honor one's own religion and con-
> demn the religions of others, but should honor oth-
> ers' religion for this or that reason. In doing so, one
> helps one's own religion grow, and renders service to
> the religion of others, too. If acting otherwise, one
> digs the grave of one's own religion, and does harm to
> other religions. Whosoever honors his own religion
> and condemns that of others does so indeed through
> devotion to his own religion, thinking, 'I will glorify
> my own religion.' But, on the contrary, in so doing he
> or she injures his or her own religion more gravely.
> So, concord is good. Let all listen and be willing to lis-
> ten to the doctrines professed by others."[1]

Dr. Desai said, "I recall a similar statement made by our late prime minister, Mr. Jawaharlal Nehru."

"Of course," I responded. "In the book, *Wit and Wisdom of Jawaharlal Nehru*, he said:

> Let us think that the truth may not perhaps be en-
> tirely with us. Let us cooperate with others, let us,
> even when we do not appreciate what others say, re-
> spect their views, and their way of life."[2]

We finally reached Dr. Desai's residence after the long drive. After lunch Dr. Desai started to question me about Buddhist tolerance of other religions. I took this opportu-nity to show various instances in which the Buddha ex-pressed tolerance.

I said, "One day Upali, a follower of Mahavira, the founder of Jainism, was sent to the Buddha to debate the theory of karma. Upali was convinced that the Buddha's theory was correct. He wanted to be a disciple of the Buddha, and he appealed to the Buddha to accept him. The Buddha advised him not to be in a hurry and to reconsider his decision. Once again, Upali begged the Buddha to accept him as a disciple. This time the Buddha advised him to continue to support and respect his former teacher as before, and then he consented to accept him as a disciple.[3]

"Gauri, do you know that the Buddha, accompanied by some of his disciples, would visit the monasteries of teachers of other religions and hold friendly discussions with them? One of those teachers came to the Buddha to have a dialogue with him. At one point in their conversation the Buddha said to him, 'You should not think that I am trying to convert you to my way. You may follow your own way. Let us discuss only the similarities between your teachings and mine.'

"Furthermore, the Buddha preached this message to his disciples.

> Monks, if outsiders should speak against me, against my teachings, or against my disciples, you should not be angry or hold that against them. If you were angry with them, how would you know if they were right or wrong? And also, if outsiders should praise me, my teachings, or my disciples, you should not be pleased or proud. If you were pleased or proud, how would you know if they were over-praising us? Therefore, whether people speak for or against me, my teachings, or my disciples, be neither proud nor angry. Rather, be impartial, and acknowledge where they are wrong. Furthermore, both anger and pride would be against your own spiritual development.[4]

"Gauri, in my opinion, for us to be happy we must accept that we are likely to have views that are not similar to the views of others. It is not easy to understand religions that are not our own. Teachings that are common to most religions are doing good deeds, avoid wrongdoing, and purifying and calming the mind. In Buddhism we are taught not to condemn other religions. It teaches us to practice tolerance and to do our best to understand other religions. This tolerance will help us live harmoniously in a multireligious world."

Gauri and Dr. Desai promised me that they would try to become more tolerant of each other's beliefs. Dr. Desai also promised that he wouldn't force Gauri to go to church unless she wanted to, and Gauri promised that if she went to church with the family, she would follow along with the ritual in a respectful manner. Gauri and her husband were able to meet each other halfway and therefore begin to lead happy lives together. After all, they did in fact love each other deeply. They are also teaching their children religious tolerance, and they sometimes bring them to the Thai temple in Chicago so that they may be exposed to the Buddhist way of life.

> If you determine your course with
> force or speed
> You miss the way of the Law.
> Quietly consider what is right and what
> is wrong.
> Receiving all opinions equally.
> Without haste, wisely observe the law.[5]

FOUR

Boundless Compassion

The telephone rang once, twice, and then thrice. When I answered, I heard an unfamiliar voice at the other end. He spoke in Sinhalese, but didn't sound fluent in the language. Then I realized he was a Sri Lankan Tamil gentleman.

Muthuswami had won a work permit when the United States government had made a certain number of "green cards" available through a lottery system. But when he arrived in Los Angeles, United States Immigration refused him entry to the country because he did not have a sponsor or money to support himself. He refused to go back to Sri Lanka, as he had arrived legally, so the only alternative was to send him to a detention camp.

Muthuswami was in a quandary. He had called a man named Joseph, whose telephone number had been given to him by one of his friends in Sri Lanka. Joseph was not in a position to help him, so Joseph gave him my telephone number, thinking that I might be able to do something for him.

I collected the necessary information and then called two Tamil gentlemen who are well known as social workers in their community in Southern California. They listened to Muthuswami's story and promised to call me back. After waiting one day and not hearing from them, I decided to give them a call. Unfortunately, they expressed no interest whatsoever in Muthuswami's case.

I decided to contact a close Tamil friend of mine to get his opinion. He encouraged me to help Muthuswami, whom he did not know personally, and he even said that he would pay legal fees if necessary.

I contacted a lawyer I knew who worked with immigration cases and handed the case over to her. She asked if I would be willing to sponsor Muthuswami and, if so, to give her an appropriate letter. Even though I didn't know Muthuswami, all I saw was a man in need of my help, so I obliged.

Two days later the attorney called me and said that I had to appear in court to vouch for Muthuswami and tell the judge that I was willing to be responsible for him. When the appointed day came, I met the attorney and Muthuswami in the courtroom. This was the first time I had actually seen him in person, even though I couldn't yet speak to him. The authorities escorted him to the defense table; he was being treated like a prisoner. When I looked at Muthuswami, I could see at once that my instincts about him had been correct. His face told me that he was an honest man with a good heart and that he would, in fact, be someone who could fit into United States society and make a positive contribution.

During the cross-examination the immigration lawyer asked me whether I was a Sinhalese or a Tamil. I replied that I was a Buddhist monk. He wanted me to answer his question, but I gave him the same answer again.

This annoyed the man, so he complained to the judge that the witness was not answering the question.

The judge addressed me directly and said, "You will please answer the question directly, sir."

I replied, "I am a Sinhalese. But since I am a Buddhist monk, I am not tied to any race."

"Explain that statement," demanded the judge.

"The Lord Buddha, who is the founder of Buddhism, told his disciples to remove all social labels once they join the order. Many rivers with different names flow into the ocean as one body of water. Furthermore, he taught us that wisdom and compassion must be the driving forces behind all our actions. He instructed us to treat all living beings with fairness and to destroy the barriers of class, creed, and race among all the peoples of the world."

The judge listened carefully and asked whether I was able to financially support Muthuswami.

"Yes, Your Honor, I am able and willing to support him," I replied.

The judge considered the matter for a few moments, and then ordered Muthuswami to be handed over to me. After the judge concluded the case, he asked me if I would stay behind for a few minutes so he could talk to me personally.

The judge approached me and said, "I was very impressed by your answers on the witness stand today. Day after day people stand before me who are victims of ideologies involving race or religion. They find themselves separated from others because of strong cultural beliefs that sometimes even lead to violence. What you spoke about today was all about inclusion and unity. This is a very important message for the world."

I replied, "In the *Metta Sutta,* or Sutta of Loving Kindness, the Buddha talks about a mother protecting her only child. He instructs us to protect every other being in a similar way. It is the way of Buddhism to demonstrate compassion and loving kindness for everyone, regardless of who or what they are or have been."

"You have made me very curious to learn more about the

Buddhist religion. Where can I get more information?" asked the judge eagerly.

The lady attorney who had represented Muthuswami spoke up and said that she would be happy to collect some literature from my temple and deliver it to the judge herself. He thanked me and said he looked forward to receiving it.

I returned to the temple with Muthuswami. I decided that I must make him feel comfortable at my temple, so I named him Raja, warning him to keep his identity as a Tamil a secret. Unfortunately, there is still a great deal of tension between the various ethnic factions in Sri Lanka.

In a few weeks I was able to find him a job. He eventually moved into his own place and saved enough money to bring his family over from Sri Lanka. He is now leading a comfortable life in Los Angeles.

Later I learned that Muthuswami was the descendant of an Indian tea picker. I reflected that perhaps it was his ancestry that was looked down upon by the Tamil social workers who showed no signs of compassion. In truth, Muthuswami is a gem of a person who is ever grateful to me for helping him out when no one else would. He is a Hindu and his wife is a Catholic, but both of them want their children to follow the compassionate path of the Buddha.

He often says to me when he comes to visit, "If it weren't for you, Bhante, I would never be able to forgive those of my own people who turned their backs on me. The compassion you showed to me is what I must now show to them. Thank you."

The following are the Buddha's words on loving kindness:[1]

> Skilled in good, wishing to attain
> a state of calm, so should one behave:
> able, upright, perfectly upright,
> open-minded, gentle, free from pride.

Contented, easily supportable,
with few duties, of right livelihood;
controlled in senses, discreet,
reserved, not greedily attached to family.

One should not commit a slight
    wrong,
that wise persons might censure,
that there be happiness and security;
may all beings be happy-minded.

Whatever beings there are,
timid, strong, and all other,
long, or huge,
average, short, or large;

Seen or unseen,
living near or far,
born or coming to birth;
may all beings be happy-minded.

Let one not deceive another,
nor despise anyone anywhere;
neither in anger nor ill will
should one wish another harm.

As a mother would risk her own life
to protect her only child,
so should one, to all living beings
cultivate a boundless heart.

Let one's love pervade the whole
world, without any obstructions,
above, below and across,
free of obstruction, enmity, hostility.

Standing, walking, sitting,
or lying down; whenever awake,
one should develop mindfulness,
as this is the highest abode.

Not falling into error, virtuous,
and endowed with insight;
giving up attachment to sense desires,
one is not again subject to birth.

FIVE

The Disciple Who
Jumped over the Cliff

The summer heat on the particular afternoon I am thinking of in August 1979 reminded me of Sri Lanka. Sauntering becomes one's speed of motion on such days. Speech slows, and the mind moves thought through gentle streams.

I had been in America a little over three years and was still experiencing occasional difficulties in adjusting to my new environment. Sri Lanka, my home temple, my venerable teachers, and the Vesak celebrations of my native country were images that continually flashed across my mind.

The Buddhist Meditation Center in Los Angeles had become my home base. As the first Theravada monk to live in the L.A. Metro area, special problems related to my uniqueness continued to arise. Sometimes I became involved in situations and encounters that opened the door for discussion, and other times the door was closed. Feeling much like an alien wherever I traveled, I felt at home and comfortable on the grounds of the BMC. There they understood at least the basic fact that I was a Buddhist monk, not a Hari Krishna devotee.

Over time, I developed a reputation for being able to give good advice on sensitive personal matters, and members of the center often sought me out for counseling. I was humbled and gratified by the respect and appreciation they showed me.

I was in my room reading on the hot August day I am thinking of, when I heard a soft but urgent knock at my door. I wondered who was behind the timid, but demanding thumping. I opened the door and there stood another resident of the meditation center, a thirty-something woman called Kamala. She was obviously very upset. I could tell that she had been crying, because her eyes were swollen and red, and her sad face told me there was a big problem.

"Oh, Bhante," she sniffed, "they told me I have to leave the center! What am I going to do? I don't have the money to move. I'm in school, but I'll have to drop out. Please tell me what I can do!"

"Please slow down, Kamala. Sit down and tell me what has happened." I had no idea why people at the center would ask her to leave.

She quickly scurried into my room as if she hoped no one would see her. "Bhante, please help me. The abbot told me to move out tonight!"

Please tell me, why were you asked to leave?"

She could only manage to speak every other word between sobs. "Bhante, Bhante, I just wanted to follow my teacher. He told me, because I gained weight. My teacher told me . . ."

"Kamala, what did your teacher say?" I asked, trying to understand her emotional mumbling. I knew that she was a follower of a popular Indian guru at the time. He was the one who had given this American girl her name, Kamala.

"Please continue, and slow down so I can understand you," I implored.

Kamala straightened up in the old sagging chair and

used her sleeve to dry her eyes. Doing her best to compose herself, she began by saying, "Bhante, I have gained a little weight lately. I asked my teacher what to do, and he advised me to have sex as often as possible—morning, noon, and night. He said that this was for my own good and that I should not think of this as sexual misconduct, but as a way of exercising to lose my unwanted weight. Since I didn't have a partner, I decided to advertise for one. I made up a bright yellow poster that said, 'Anyone who needs sex, please contact me.' I signed it 'Kamala.' I put the poster up on the wall in the dining room, and another one near the door to my room. The abbot was having breakfast the next morning when he saw it. I heard he almost choked on his cereal! There it was, right in front of him. Bhante, I'm telling you, he is really upset! He told me to move out immediately. What am I to do? I have to follow my teacher's advice, but if I do, I will have to move. I have always followed my teacher's advice to the letter. Am I to disobey my guru? No matter how difficult it is, I will follow him anywhere he leads me, and I will do whatever he tells me to do!" The rest of her words were drowned out by tears.

I couldn't believe my ears. "Kamala! Would you jump off a cliff if your teacher told you to? You have to think for yourself!" I warned her. "Do you think that in having a teacher, or in following a teaching, that you should give up your mind? Is a teacher there to lean on and follow blindly, or to teach you to walk by yourself? It is absolute foolishness to follow another's wisdom without the judgment of his or her own understanding."

Her teary eyes began to clear up, and her face bore a question mark.

I continued forcefully, "You don't have to surrender your will to anyone, including a teacher. You must listen to your own inner voice and discover your own truth. Even the Buddha urged the monks to question authority. In the

Mahaparinibbana Sutta, he gives the following examples. One *bhikkhu* is quoted as saying, 'I heard and learned it from the Blessed One's own lips.' Another *bhikkhu* said, 'I heard and learned it from the lips of the Blessed One's community of closest disciples.' A third, learned *bhikkhu* said, 'I am the master of the Blessed One's teaching, and I also consulted all of the recognized experts on the Blessed One's teaching. I heard it from the lips of those experts.' Finally, a group of *bhikkhus* said, 'We are the experts in the Blessed One's teachings. Ours is the truth, and you must listen to us.'[1]

"You must realize that each of these monks declared his version to be the law, his discipline to be the correct discipline, his teaching to be the true teaching of the Master, but the statements of each of the monks should not be believed without first comparing them to the Buddha's original doctrines."

Her sobs were beginning to subside, and she began to calm down. I continued.

"The Buddha himself, the Enlightened One, attributed all his realization, attainments, and achievements to human intelligence and human endeavor. He said, 'One is one's own refuge; who else could be the refuge?'[2] He admonished his disciples to be a refuge unto themselves and never to seek shelter in, or help from, anybody else. Kamala, as is true of all people, you have the power to develop yourself, to work for your own freedom, to liberate yourself from all bondage. The Buddha says 'You should do your own work, for the Tathagatas only teach us the Way.'[3] Your emancipation depends on your own discovery of Truth, for you must be the one to see; no one can see for you. If you were blind, could I really describe the color blue to you? I could give you an idea, but you would have to experience it yourself to really know what it looks like.[4]

"If this were not true, then why wouldn't the great

teachers throughout time have liberated all people simply with their own will? The Buddha taught that in using your own rational mind, if you see that a teaching is wholesome, then accept it wholeheartedly; if it is unwholesome, then discard it immediately.

"There is an old story about the Buddha visiting a town called Kesaputta. The residents of the town were called Kalamas. They welcomed the Buddha as he walked into their midst, and they had a desire to ask him about the various teachers that had visited Kesaputta.

"'Sir, one teacher comes and explains their doctrine, asking that we scorn and denounce others' doctrines. Then another teacher comes along and expounds his own doctrine, also asking that we scorn and denounce the others' doctrines. This goes on and on with various gurus and *brahmanas*. But we are in doubt and we are perplexed as to who among these teachers spoke the truth and who spoke falsehood.'

"The Buddha responded by saying, 'Yes, Kalamas, it is proper that you have a doubt, that you have perplexity, for a doubt has arisen in a matter that is doubtful. Do not be led by reports or tradition or hearsay. Do not be led by the authority of religious texts, or by mere logic or inference, or by considering appearances or by delight in speculative opinions, or by seeming possibilities, or by the mere fact that it is your very own teacher who told you. But, O Kalamas, when you know within yourselves that certain things are blameworthy, are condemned by the wise, and are conducive to harm and suffering, then you should abandon them at once. On the other hand, when you know within yourselves that certain things are without blame and are, in fact, good things, then accept and follow them without delay.'⁵

"Remember," I continued, "as long as there is doubt and perplexity, no progress is possible. It is also undeniable that there must be doubt as long as you do not understand or see things clearly. But in order to progress it is absolutely necessary to rid yourself of doubt and be able to see things exactly as they are. The Buddha instructed us that after placing our trust in a good person, it is not necessary to accept everything that person says merely on the basis of faith. We all need the guidance of our teachers, but that doesn't mean that we have to follow them blindly. We must use our rational mind. Also, if we accept something on the basis of good faith, that we do not yet completely understand, while at the same time remaining open to what is yet to unfold, we must examine very carefully the method that was used to determine if it is true or false. The Buddha himself said that eventually we must even discard the *dhamma*. He reminded us that the *dhamma* is like a raft. He said that once one has crossed the river, it would be a burden to carry a raft that is no longer needed.[6] Your understanding of the meaning of what you do must be deeper than the mere ritual of doing it. This is your lesson, Kamala."

Her face relaxed a bit and I could tell that she was beginning to grasp what I had explained to her. "Do you know the meaning of your name?"

"Not really, Bhante."

"Your name, 'Kamala,' means lotus, which symbolizes purity. Remember that the lotus grows in deep mud. It surfaces through the unclean water of the pond and blossoms forth gloriously, a beautiful sight for everyone to appreciate and enjoy. A human being can be compared to a lotus. He or she may be born in an environment of unfavorable circumstances. The water in the pond can be a metaphor for the society in which the individual grows. Regardless of one's birth and upbringing, the individual, like the lotus, is able to emerge into society without surrendering to harmful or unwholesome influences."[7]

She began to see the truth of what I had said. The realization of her foolishness finally began to dawn on her, and she started to laugh at herself with the full force of her embarrassment.

"Bhante, how could I have put up that sign? I can't believe I actually did that! No wonder the abbot wants me out of here! Do you think he could ever forgive me? I was so stupid to follow my teacher so literally and interpret his words so incorrectly. I really do believe I can find another way to lose weight!" She was laughing so hard by this time that I thought she might fall out of her chair.

"Don't worry, Kamala," I reassured her, "I will speak to the abbot on your behalf. I will explain to him that you have learned a lesson yourself—in addition to understanding the virtue of practicing sexual purity."

She looked at me with an innocent look in her eyes that told me she would do her best to pay attention to the guidance of her own *inner* teacher. I did, in fact, speak to the abbot later that day, and by the evening, the *unwelcome* mat was removed from her door.

Another day in America had passed, and once again I had had the opportunity to contemplate how much alike people are all around the world. I reflected on the fact that it is easy for people to be unknowingly misled, and even brainwashed, by irrational beliefs and false teachers. How important is this lesson of the Buddha reminding us to rely only on our own experience to interpret the facts, to make our own decisions, and to determine our own truths.

By the way, Kamala eventually developed a very analytical mind and decided not to follow in the footsteps of her guru. To this day she is a devout, practicing Buddhist.

> Oneself is one's own protector;
> What other protector can there be?
> With oneself fully controlled,

One obtains a protection, which is hard
    to gain.
Do not follow mean things.
Do not dwell in negligence.
Do not embrace false views.
Be watchful.
Be not heedless.
Follow the Law of Virtue.
The virtuous live happily in this world
    now and also hereafter.[8]

SIX

The Punks Meet the Monk

On this particular summer afternoon, the Los Angeles smog hung like a painter's shroud, and an eerie stillness impregnated the entire area. A thought arose: such days are for writing, stillness, or walks at the ocean's edge.

The phone rang for the umpteenth time that day. It was Sara.

Sara called often of late. Her daughter, Becky, who was captured by the thrills of drug addiction, had given up the responsibility of her son, Mike, to her mother. Becky had suddenly delivered him to Sara one day, seemingly without much concern and with few comments. It seemed that life's shadow was infiltrating the deepest levels of Becky's being, and Sara had become a new mother due to these circumstances.

"How 'bout going to the pier for a walk with me?" asked Sara over the phone. That day had turned out to be busier than most, but I knew that Sara needed someone to talk to about her daughter's problem. Even though I was pressed for time, I decided that a trip down to the beach would give me an opportunity to counsel her. "I'll be ready in a half hour," I responded. "Come get me."

Sara and little Mike arrived with baseball caps and sunny dispositions. We headed out to Santa Monica for our stroll down the pier. The ride to the beach was another opportunity to listen and support Sara in one of the most difficult moments of her life. She had gained a grandson, but felt that she had lost a daughter to drugs. She bounced like a ball between the joy of Mike's laughter and the sadness of her heart, hoping to learn a way to balance the agitation of her mind, regardless of the up and down swings of her emotions.

Suddenly, there before us, lay the ocean in all its azure beauty. The horizon seemed to beckon us to a farther look. The boundary between the sky and the water disappeared into a sparkling dance of light, and the seagulls seemed to move with the ballet. I took a deep breath of coastal air. Sara yawned and took it all in, pleased to see little Mike's excitement at seeing the ocean for the first time.

"Last one there's a rotten egg," shouted Sara. She looked as free as a bird. Sara and Mike hopped out of the car and ran off toward the pier. I followed slowly.

"Come on!" Mike shouted to me. "Race you to the pier!"

I caught up with him, and as we approached the sand, an odd sight caught my eye. Running toward us like a herd of buffalos, were five young men and women, dressed in rags, with purple hair. We slowed and steadied ourselves and veered to the side of the boardwalk. Sara exclaimed, "Bhante, look what's coming! What is it? Do you see what I see?"

By then I was beginning to see them more clearly, and from where I stood, they didn't seem like the welcoming types. We looked at one another for some direction, but could come up with nothing to say. We gradually slowed to a crawling pace about ten feet from the motley crew.

I must say that I found these folks quite interesting, and any fear I might have felt was temporarily diverted by my curiosity. The young man in the middle had a hairstyle that looked like the quills of a porcupine! His hair stood straight up as if he had inserted some body part into an electrical outlet. The sides of his head were shaven so as to accent the effect. The brilliant and numerous colors of his shirt would surely be an eye opener for any late riser. As for his friends, they seemed to have graduated from the same fashion school. As the shock and marvel at their neochic statement began to fade, I once again became aware that this group didn't appear to be all that friendly.

"Hey, look there," one of the electrically shocked young persons proclaimed. "Looks like we got us a shaved pumpkin! Why, he don't even got no hair."

These comments seemed to be heading in a negative direction, I began to think. As the group continued to move closer, the three of us froze. The only movement came from Sara, as she clutched Mike closer to her. The porcupine leader stepped in front of me as if to block my way, even though I was as still as a rock. I was hoping to be as soft as a flower, although I had images of one recently plucked.

The group became more inquisitive and probing. "Hey, I bet this is a real live alien! What planet are you from, buddy?" The finger-pointing turned into a light round of pushing. "You got some alien ID?"

I was trying to remain calm, or at least to appear so. Inside, the images of picked flowers started to look more like crushed ones. My mind reached for a diversion—any diversion. Before I even knew what to say, I started speaking.

"Are you guys punkies?" I asked as politely as I could.

"What's he mean, *punkies*? Punk-*ees*!??" They started to laugh at this alien's pronunciation. "You mean punks, don't you?"

"Oh, is that what you call yourselves?" I replied. "Punks. Hmm. Did you know that I'm a new kind of punk?"

This startling question seemed to momentarily give them pause.

"Yes, I'm the new kind of punk," I continued with caution.

"You guys are the old style, and I'm the new style of punk. Look here. You have all kinds of colored clothing, but I have one color, bright yellow. But honestly, I'm not attached to any colors. And look. You shave the sides of your head, but I've shaved my entire head. See? I am the new punk!"

They had completely stopped in their tracks, either in amazement at my sheer gall, or because they were trying to figure out if I was dangerously insane or just plain strange. In any case, it compelled them to focus and start to listen. I knew I had them then, and I didn't want to lose their attention.

"Hey guys, just look at me. No hair. Bright yellow robes. I'm a real punk!"

While they continued to stare, I reached out my hand in friendship. "Hello, my name is Bhante. Bhante Piyananda."

"Piy-a-what?" one of the girls responded.

"Bhante, for spiritual friend. *Piya* means pleasant and *ananda* means happy one. So, I am your pleasant and happy spiritual friend!"

The girl smiled. "Hey, that sounds good! My name is Ana." It seemed to me that the iceberg was finally beginning to melt.

"Hmm, Bhante. Well, they call me Gopher," one of the young men uttered. They began to introduce themselves in colorful terms. "I'm known as Binko." "I'm Bear." "I'm Wild Sister," said the girl with the tattoos and pierced eyebrows.

The colorful group joined Sara, Mike, and me, and we all continued our walk toward the beach.

We stopped for a moment and I pointed to the ocean, remarking that there are lessons we can learn from the sea.

"What kind of lessons can we learn from the dumb ocean?" asked Ana very aggressively.

"Well, do you know how to swim?"

"Of course we know, Dumbo."

"When you had your first lesson swimming in the ocean, did you go to the deep sea right away?"

"No way, Jose," she replied.

"You started at the shallow waters by the beach, right? And gradually swam out to where you couldn't touch bottom."

Ana nodded, "Yes."

"So you see, there is a gradual process in learning. Throughout our lives we learn to educate ourselves in stages, with patience."[1]

"You sound like my parents. They want me to be a doctor, but I'll never be able to do that," she said, with a look of self-doubt on her heavily made-up face.

"Never be able to do what, Ana?" I asked.

"When I read the course of studies I would have to take to become a doctor, I felt nervous and afraid. No way could I go to college for eight to ten years. I'm just not smart enough."

"Think about not only swimming in the ocean, but about climbing to the top of a high mountain. If you go to the base of the mountain and look at the top, you will definitely be afraid to climb it, and you will think that you could never get to the summit. But if you climb gradually and steadily, you will eventually reach the top. This applies to any undertaking."

"That's enough about swimming and mountain climbing. What else can you teach us about the ocean?" questioned Gopher.

"The ocean is fixed and does not go past its shores. In the same manner, we should stay within the boundaries of our societal ethics and not become a burden or a menace to our people."

"What do you mean by 'societal ethics'?" Gopher asked with a puzzled expression.

"Well, let me explain a few things," I responded patiently. "First of all, we should know how to talk to each other, because communication is the basis of friendship. Speech plays a very important part in all human relations. It can promote truth, harmony, and peace. It can also create misunderstanding, discord, and falsehood. We should always remember to think before we open our mouths."

"Think about what?" asked Gopher, becoming interested.

"You have to ask yourself the following questions:

> Do I speak the truth?
> Do I speak gently?
> Are my words beneficial to others?
> Do I speak out of goodwill?
> Do I speak at the proper time and place?"[2]

"That's an awful lot to think about before saying anything," remarked Gopher with a grin.

They all started to laugh, except Wild Sister, who was busy reapplying her makeup using a hand mirror.

"What is the purpose of that mirror?" I asked her.

"So I can see myself, of course," she replied, looking at me as if I was a moron.

"All right. Then in the same way, we have to look at our actions, words, and thoughts as if they were being reflected in a mirror. Before we act, we have to think about whether or not our actions are harmful to ourselves or to others. If they are beneficial to someone, by all means, go ahead and act."

"Oh! So you are trying to teach me how to think! Tell me something else that's useful," said Wild Sister sarcastically.

"Let me explain, many rivers bearing particular names

will flow into the ocean. Once the water mingles with the ocean it all becomes one. We cannot differentiate one drop from the other. In the same manner, people of different faiths, cultures, and traditions come to America and eventually infuse into one society."

"Then tell us exactly what you are—since we know you're not an alien," said porcupine Gopher, with an even wider grin, and by now very curious.

"I'm a Buddhist monk, and as I said, people call me Bhante, yet any sort of label is immaterial. Remember the line from Shakespeare, 'What's in a name? That which we call a rose, by any other name would smell as sweet.' We, like the ocean, must overcome the barriers of class, creed, race, religion, and other differences and learn to develop a universal love for all people, which will help us live harmonious lives. The ocean is the home of many kinds of fish of all sizes and shapes. They have equal opportunities to survive, don't you think?"

"I don't agree," shouted Binko. "The big fish eat the small fish."

"That's the American way," they all chimed in.

"The small fish, if they are smart enough, can evade the predator and survive," I said. "In my country we say, 'One's own hand to one's own head.' One is one's own refuge; if you want to do anything in life, you must persevere so as to accomplish your goal."

"That's interesting," responded Binko. "Tell us more about the ocean."

"The rivers bring all types of debris into the ocean. The ocean waves discard it on the shore. In the same manner, we must discard our impure thoughts, which are harbored deep inside ourselves. These impure thoughts are usually generated by anger, hatred, and jealousy. You should immediately discards these sorts of thoughts whenever they arise in your mind."

"Well, that's easier said than done," said Wild Sister. "My biggest problem is my parents. They are a total pain in the behind, and I can't stop myself from hating them."

"Well, I understand your feelings, yet your parents are two people you can never, ever repay for the gift of life they have given you." I paused to let this thought sink in for a moment.

"I'm tired of walking. Let's sit over here," suggested Ana. So we made ourselves comfortable on the sand.

"Parents do a great many things for their children. They bring them up, they give them nourishment, they introduce them to the world, and they do what they can to protect them. Your parents were also your first teachers."

"But my mother always punished me for the smallest things," Wild Sister complained with bitterness in her voice.

"Can you remember why she punished you?" I asked.

She paused for a moment to think. "One day I didn't come home until 4:00 A.M. My cranky mother spanked me and grounded me for a month. I don't see what I did wrong. What do you say about that?" she asked angrily.

"My dear child, if you were choking and your mother gave you a big slap on the back, is this to hurt you or to save your life? I believe that your mother tried to teach you how to be a good girl, and she probably worried about you when you didn't come home until 4:00 A.M. She probably couldn't even get to sleep until you got home. She undoubtedly grounded you because she loves you. She wanted to teach you about personal responsibility and caring about the people who care for you."

Wild Sister looked down at the ground when she heard this, and I could tell that she felt sad about her mother and the way she had treated her.

Binko then spoke up and said, "My big problem is my stepfather. He abused me when I was a kid. He used to hit me and do even worse things to me. He hit my mother, too, and I was powerless to do anything about it. I can never forgive him." When he said this last sentence, he clenched his teeth and pounded his fist in the sand.

"Binko, even though he mistreated you, you must somehow learn how to forgive your stepfather. Let go of your thoughts of ill will and revenge. I know you feel you would like to get back at him for what he did to you and your mother, but nothing will change the past. Right now you are drowning in your hatred. And it is only by forgiving him that you will be saved from drowning. Your hatred could eventually make you, yourself, just as hard and equally as abusive as the stepfather you hate. This is how this pattern repeats itself from generation to generation. Forgiveness will allow you to make room in your heart for positive feelings—like patience and love. Hatred is never overcome by more hatred. It is only love that can replace hate.[3] Remember this: hate restricts, while love releases; hate divides, while love unites. The ocean never keeps the garbage and debris that is thrown into it. We have to become like the ocean and throw our hatred onto the shore of forgiveness."

"Bhante, you are a very good story teller. I like the way you talk about the ocean. Please tell us some more," said Gopher.

By this time we were all feeling very comfortable with one another, and I was pleased that the feeling was getting to be very friendly. Even Sara and Mike were beginning to warm up to our formerly hostile companions. They just sat there calmly and watched and listened, not sure at all about the outcome, but no longer feeling threatened.

I continued. "It can rain for years and years at a time, but the ocean will never flood, yes? Or, there can be no rain for years and years at a time, but the ocean will never run dry. Isn't this also true? In the same manner, the human being may be praised again and again, but if he were wise, he wouldn't become proud and haughty, which would be like a flood. By the same token, the human being may be unrightfully blamed again and again, but, if he were wise, he would avoid becoming depressed and unhappy, which would be like running dry.

"To an optimist, the world looks absolutely rosy, and to a pessimist the world looks absolutely grim. But the truth is, life is constantly changing, it is forever impermanent. In one's lifetime one can experience gain, loss, fame, praise, blame, happiness, and pain. It is also very possible to have each of these experiences more than once.[4]

"Is that all, Bhante? Anything else you can tell us?" asked Gopher.

"Of course, if you have time to listen. The ocean depths contain a vast amount of treasure—most of it unknown and unseen. In the same way, you have vast amounts of treasure within you, and it is also unknown and unseen. This treasure within you is your potential.

"The human is the highest living being in the world. In Buddhism, we believe that to be born a human is a very fortunate thing. It is only human beings who can discover the treasures within themselves and reach the depths of their oceans of potential."

"Bhante, what you've told us is very interesting. And I want you to know that, personally, I have no prejudice against you. But how can I believe what you are telling me and not go against the God I was brought up to believe in?" questioned Ana.

"Well Ana, this will be my last lesson about the ocean. All over the world the ocean water is salty, right? The water here in Santa Monica is just as salty as the water in my homeland of Sri Lanka. By the same token, what you call God, I call good. I just add an extra *o*, but we both mean the same thing. In actuality, they are only different terms, but just as salty. Do you see? I believe that religious leaders everywhere, whether they teach about 'God' or teach about 'good,' work to help their people lead better lives. They all teach us to do good things and to be good people, thus leading godly lives."

"You sound cool, Bhante, and we like talking with you. When can we see you again?" asked Bear, who had heretofore been the silent one.

"Please come to my temple, which is on Crenshaw and Washington Boulevard. Here is my card. I will be more than willing to answer all your future questions, about the ocean or anything else you might have in mind."

"Thank you," they echoed in chorus.

One by one they turned to Sara and Mike and thanked them for coming down to the beach that day with Punkie Monkie, as I would always be known to them. Then they turned and walked away from us, their curiously colored hairstyles shining in the bright sunshine.

"Sara, I'm sorry our day at the beach didn't turn out the way you wanted it to. I had no idea we would encounter such unexpected visitors," I remarked to my friend.

"Never mind, Bhante. I learned more about the ocean today than I would ever have learned if you hadn't met these young people. From listening to you, I realized that in the same way as the ocean can never hold onto anything dirty that is thrown into it, I can't hold onto the anger I feel toward my daughter. I need to begin practicing patience and forgiveness toward her or Mike will carry these feelings with him into yet another generation. I also think that it was a good experience for Mike to meet such unlikely individuals as we encountered here today."

Mike turned up to me and yelled, "Punkie Monkie!"

Sara and I laughed out loud, then shook off the sand and started walking back toward the car. You might be surprised to know that all five of the beach group did in fact visit me at my temple, and three of them became my students. One of them even became a Buddhist minister and still keeps in touch with me.

> Let the discerning person guard the
>   mind,
> So difficult to detect and extremely
>   subtle,
> Seizing whatever it desires.
> A guarded mind brings happiness.[5]

SEVEN

The Balancing Act

On the day of the full moon in May, Buddhists throughout the world celebrate Vesak, the anniversary of the Lord Buddha's birth, enlightenment, and *paranibbana*, or passing into *nibbana*. In 1985, I was graciously invited by my friend Bhante Seela to attend the Vesak celebrations in Berkeley, sponsored by the Northern California Sangha Council and the Buddhist community. I had known Bhante Seela since my days as a youth in Sri Lanka, and I was very happy to accept his invitation.

I decided to make the trip north from Los Angeles with two of our resident monks, Bhante Sumedha and Bhante Nanda. As spring was upon the land, we knew that the vistas from the car would be grand. And they were! Such flowering fields we had not seen before.

We arrived in Berkeley midafternoon, during the first meeting. The Sangha Council was holding a planning session at 3:00 P.M., and Bhante Sumedha, Nanda, and I had just enough time for a visit to the men's room, which we learned was located in the basement. Bhante Sumedha and

Nanda headed down before me, and I followed a few minutes later. Some of the students remembered me from a previous visit, and they stopped me to ask questions. By the time I got down to the basement I was in a bit of a hurry.

As I walked down the stairs I noticed a woman leaning against the ladies' room door with a strained looked on her face. As I approached to pass her, she smiled in a friendly manner and asked me if I was a Hari Krishna. This was not an unusual question for me, and I was never offended by the inquiry. But still, I was in a hurry to make it to the beginning of the meeting upstairs at 3:00 P.M.

"No, I am not," I replied in a bit of a rushed manner. "I am a Buddhist monk."

The woman quickly replied, "Oh great, then I can trust you."

For a fleeting moment I thought about the odd turn this conversation was taking.

Then she promptly said, "Could you do me a favor?"

I was beginning to wonder just *what* she had in mind.

The woman had not moved, although I could sense her discomfort, and I was uneasily anticipating what might come next.

Then she said something that completely threw me for a loop! "Sir," she began, "could you please come to the bathroom and help me remove my pants?"

I had never been in such a situation before!

The look on my face must have startled her, and she quickly hurried forward to thrust her arms toward me.

Standing before me was quite a sight, indeed. As she raised her arms, I could see that they were both wrapped in white plaster casts, up beyond her elbows. Then I immediately noticed that her dress was wet and that she wasn't able to remove her clothing in order to use the bathroom. A wave of compassion suddenly overcame my hurriedness, doubts, and confusion.

But what was I to do? I know that nature calls and that she desperately needed to use the bathroom. Poor thing, I thought. But how can I, as a Buddhist monk, go into the women's bathroom and help her?

The next day's imaginary newspaper headlines flashed before my mind's eye: "Buddhist Monk Found with Naked Woman in Ladies' Room at Vesak Celebrations." Oh boy! Then CBS news. Sri Lankan newspapers. Scandal. Security guards taking me away. Lawyers. Press conferences. All of that crossed my mind and snowballed into a complete disaster. But, then again, I couldn't just leave her there to suffer!

Then I remembered that there was a sizable gathering upstairs and that I might be able to call upon someone for help. I immediately asked the woman to wait just a moment, and spontaneously placed my monk's bag at her feet. I quickly ran up the stairs.

I spotted a Latin American lady I knew named Mary. She was the wife of a member of the Sri Lankan community. I said, "Mary, come quick. There's a lady downstairs who needs your help right away!"

Mary followed me immediately with no questions asked.

We got downstairs and Mary sized up the situation at once. She quickly put her arms around the desperate woman and led her into the ladies' room.

The point is, it was important to help this lady in need and to feel compassion for her dire circumstances. But it was also important for me to remain clearheaded and handle the situation skillfully. If compassion had been my only guide, I would probably have become the monthly feature story in a number of national gossip magazines. On the other hand, if I had not sought to assist this poor woman, she would have been left in a horrible condition without anyone to help her. So thinking fast, and balancing all the outcomes on the scale at once, become the keys to creating results that work for everyone.

There is an old story about how a bird is able to fly. If a bird has no wings it won't be able to fly and will surely crash to the ground. Also, if a bird has no eyes, but it does have wings, he may be able to fly, but he will soon hit trees or buildings and will also crash to the ground. It is possible to liken a bird's wings to compassion and a bird's eyes to wisdom or skillfulness. A bird needs both wings and eyes in order to fly, and a human needs both compassion and wisdom, or skillfulness, in order to navigate the currents of life and be successful.

The Buddha said that in order to be a responsible member of society we should develop the five faculties of: faith (*saddha*), wisdom (*panna*), energy (*viriya*), concentration (*samadhi*), and mindfulness (*sati*).[1]

Faith and wisdom are a pair of faculties that should be developed equally. A person with too much faith but lacking in wisdom will become blind and foolish. On the other hand, one who has too much knowledge without the balancing element of faith will become cold and insensitive. Too much faith can cause one to become blind to one's circumstances.[2] I can illustrate this through one of my experiences.

When I was a young monk in Sri Lanka, I lived in a temple in a small village. One day I was walking behind my teacher to visit a person who was ill. It is a tradition in my country to venerate Buddhist monks. Whenever a monk passes by, the lay people stand aside to pay their respects. Sometimes they approach the monks, put their hands together as in prayer, and bow before them. The people are happy to do this.

This particular day, as we were passing a devotee's house, a woman stopped sweeping the ground with her broom, came running toward us, braced the broom against my teacher's shoulder, and prostrated herself before him. I chuckled under my breath at the sight of this blind faith.

The woman had inadvertently propped the broom up against the monk's shoulder, completely blind to the fact that this act was highly disrespectful—while at the same time attempting to pay her respects by prostrating herself on the ground!

Too much wisdom and lack of faith makes one doubtful and unstable. One tends to question oneself in every situation. Therefore, faith and wisdom must be equally balanced.

Furthermore, the second pair of faculties, concentration and energy, should also be balanced equally. Energy is more productive when it is balanced with concentration. The Buddha says it's like catching a quail with your hand. If we use too much energy, the quail will be squeezed to death; if we don't apply enough energy, it will fly through our fingers.

On another occasion the Buddha had a discussion with a monk named Sona. Here he compared the balancing of effort to the tuning of a musical instrument. Sona was an energetic monk who meditated all day, but could not develop his concentration. Then he decided to give up his robe and return to his lay life as a musician. The Buddha appeared before him and said, "I heard you were a well-known lute player before you became a monk. Is this true?"

"Yes, my Lord."

"When the strings were too *tight,* was the lute melodious and playable?" asked the Buddha.

"No, my Lord," replied Sona.

"When the strings were too *loose,* was the lute melodious and playable?"

"No, Lord."

The Buddha then asked, "When the strings were neither too tight, nor too loose, was the lute melodious and playable?"

"Yes, Lord Buddha, when they are properly balanced, the music is sweet and melodious."[3]

Then the Buddha explained, "It is the same with our effort. When it is either too eager or too lax, the result of our effort will be lacking. But if we are to follow the Middle Path and develop balance in our mind, the result of our effort will be satisfactory. Furthermore, we should practice the Middle Path in all of our everyday activities, using mindfulness as our overriding guide."

Faith and wisdom, energy and concentration, are the two pairs of faculties that function best when in perfect balance. The fifth faculty of mindfulness stands alone and must be present every moment, whether or not the two pairs are in or out of balance. Mindfulness is the element that keeps the two pairs in check. Mindfulness is the ingredient in the formula without which the entire organism malfunctions. Mindfulness is the scale upon which the two pairs weigh in as balanced and function with each other in perfect symmetry.

Thus, to lead a successful life, there must always be a balance between wisdom and faith, effort and concentration, each pair functioning within a state of total and complete mindfulness.

> Let one not neglect one's own welfare
> For the sake of another, however great.
> Clearly understanding one's own
> welfare,
> Let one be intent upon the good.[4]

EIGHT

Karmic Ties

While I was studying at Northwestern University in Chicago, which is a Methodist-supported university, I lived in residential quarters called the Garrett with Methodist seminary students. My classmates were all amazed that I had a clean-shaven head and wore my thin saffron robe even in severe winter. I was the only Buddhist monk on campus, so I aroused curiosity wherever I went.

One day on my way to the library, a young girl approached me. "Excuse me, sir. Do you mind if I speak with you?" she asked.

"Not at all," I replied with a smile.

"My name is Diana, and I was wondering if you could tell me what kind of religion you belong to." She had a very likable manner, and I appreciated her directness with me.

"I am from Sri Lanka, Diana, and I am a Buddhist monk. I follow the teachings of Gautama Buddha."

"I don't know very much about the Buddha. Can you tell me more?" she asked.

I was very happy to meet someone who was so interested

in Buddhism, so I proceeded to explain. "Gautama Buddha was born as Prince Siddhartha in North India, in the city of Lumbini in present-day Nepal. He was married, had a son, and lived a life of luxury, never even aware of the severe hardships and sufferings of his fellow human beings. One day, however, he went outside the palace walls and was confronted with the reality of life and saw the suffering of mankind. He decided at that time to seek a solution for this suffering. So, Diana, at the age of twenty-nine, he left his kingdom and became an ascetic, a wandering, penniless monk."

Diana seemed to be interested in the story I was telling her, so I continued.

"He wandered as an ascetic for six years, following the teachings and practices of various teachers. During this time he also practiced self-mortification, causing his physical body to become weak and emaciated. Eventually, seeing that he had nearly destroyed his body, he came to the realization that neither self-mortification nor a life of luxury will help a human being on the path of purification. This realization caused the Buddha to follow what he called the Middle Path, which is midway between the two extremes."

At this point Diana said, "Did he have a teacher who told him about the Middle Path?"

"No, Diana, at this point the Buddha had left all his teachers behind. The realization of the Middle Path was attained completely through his own effort and insight. One day during his thirty-fifth year, Gautama was seated under a bodhi tree and attained enlightenment. After this experience he was known as the Buddha, or the Enlightened One, and he shared the realization of his truth with students for the next forty-five years. He taught all classes of men and women, kings and peasants, never discriminating in any way."[1]

"So what is Buddhism, anyway? Is it only the story of Gautama's life?" she asked.

"No, Diana, it is much more than that. Buddhism is a

philosophy, a way of life, and a formalized religion. Buddhism teaches us to develop compassion and wisdom and the ability to see life as it really is. Practicing Buddhism helps one improve one's relationships in the family, as well as in the community. Buddhism emphasizes self-reliance as the means to achieve one's goals. It teaches one to be tolerant toward other religions and to show loving kindness and compassion toward all living beings."

"Thank you so much for taking the time to tell me about Buddhism. May I have your name, please, so I'll know what to call you if I see you again around campus?"

"My name is Walpola Piyananda, and I am a student here, too."

"How can I learn more about Buddhism?" she asked, genuinely interested.

"Tomorrow I have free time from ten to noon. Why don't you meet me in the teaching assistants' office at the Department of Religion?"

"I sure will," replied Diana.

The next day, Diana visited me as promised. She seemed quite eager to hear me, and I did my best to make her comfortable in my office.

"How do I address you?" she asked, smiling.

"You can call me Bhante, which means 'spiritual friend.'"

"Bhante, could you tell me the essence of Buddhism?"

"With pleasure. I will first explain the Four Noble Truths, on which the religion is based. They are

> The Truth of Suffering
> The Truth of the Cause of Suffering
> The Truth of the End of Suffering
> The Truth of the Path Leading to the End
>   of Suffering[2]

"Suffering? Do you mean that all of us are suffering?" asked Diana, not sure at all what this meant.

"Diana, suffering, or *dukkha*, in Pali, actually has no exact English equivalent word. In my view, the closest translation would be 'extreme dissatisfaction with circumstances.' I will explain this further. If people examine their own experience, they will see that life is full of suffering, or of circumstances with which they are dissatisfied. The suffering may be physical, mental, or emotional. For example, it would be mental or emotional suffering to be separated from your loved ones, to see your aged parents in pain, or to face recurring financial or relationship problems. Examples of physical suffering would include pain associated with disease, disability, or accident. Even a small headache could be called physical suffering during the moment one is experiencing it.

"According to Buddhism the direct causes of suffering are desire, craving, or ignorance. This includes not only the desire for the pleasures of the senses, but the desire to cling to life as well."[3]

"I have a desire to graduate," replied Diana with a smile. "Do you think it is wrong to desire something like that?"

"No, a desire to graduate from university is not an inappropriate desire, but it would depend on your *intention* as to why you want to graduate. If it is only a means to satisfy your senses and your ego, then it is inappropriate. If your desire is to be a good citizen, to help yourself, your family, and your society—then it is a useful desire."

"Bhante, I am confused. . . ." I could see by the look on her face that she was trying her best to understand what I was saying.

"Let me explain further, Diana, as I know this subject is not easy to digest. When people are ignorant and in the dark spiritually, they develop a constant craving for certain pleasures that they believe will satisfy their inner longings. These pleasures are ephemeral and do not last. Very soon, those who become dependent on these pleasures become restless and will stoop to any level to maintain the source of those pleasures; such is the case with drug addicts, for instance.

Diana looked at me quizzically, and then said, "That means that in Buddhism there is no happiness, right?"

"Of course there is happiness in Buddhism. When one learns to remove desire and ignorance, one achieves happiness. I remember the Buddha's words from the Dhammapada:

> Health is the greatest gain,
> Contentment is the greatest wealth,
> A trusted friend is the best relative,
> Nirvana is the highest happiness."[4]

"Bhante, please tell me how I can achieve this happiness." Diana was definitely being as sincere as she could be.

"The Buddha discovered the causes of suffering and implemented cures for them. These cures give physical, mental, and emotional relief. The explanation is in the Fourth Noble Truth, which is comprised of the Noble Eightfold Path."

"Tell me about the Eightfold Path," she requested.

"The Noble Eightfold Path is the Middle Path, which avoids the two extremes: indulgence in the pleasures of the senses, and mortification of the flesh. At first, as I have already said, a person will usually seek happiness through the pleasures of the senses. These pleasures inevitably lead to desire, which eventually takes a firm hold on the mind. The other extreme is the practice of self-mortification, or the inflicting of pain and torture on one's own mind and body."

"Could you please explain in a simple way what you just said?" asked Diana, obviously a bit confused.

"Diana, let's assume that an individual craves food all the time. He may have a very high metabolism—or a serious condition like bulimia. On the other hand, one may

suppress their appetite for food and refrain from eating because they think they are overweight—and eventually become anorexic. We must avoid these two extremes in order
to maintain balance in our lives. Therefore, the Eightfold
Path teaches us to avoid these two extremes, and guides us
on the path of moderation."[5]

"Not only those two, Bhante, but what about the extreme views of people?"

"You are absolutely correct, Diana. There are extremists
of all kinds, be they political, racial, religious, or social.
They believe that only their views are correct. Our Buddhist
practice is the path of moderation and flexibility. We are
willing to listen and consider others' viewpoints before
making up our minds about any given situation."

Diana seemed enthusiastic and asked me what the
Eightfold Path was.

I continued, "The first step is Right Understanding,
which is usually arrived at through analytical observation.
Right Understanding is seeing things as they truly are.
In order to do this, one must first observe one's self and
one's situation and comprehend the meaning of what is
observed.

"The second aspect is Right Thought. Thoughts always
influence our words and actions. Right Thought means to
avoid desire and ill will and to cultivate thoughts of selfless
renunciation, loving kindness, and compassion. We must
learn to forgive and not to harbor anger."

"It sounds practical to me," said Diana with appreciation.

"Yes, Diana, it is very practical. Listen to this quotation
from the Dhammapada:

> He abused me, he hit me, he oppressed me, he
> robbed me. Those who continue to hold such
> thoughts never still their hatred. For in this world,

hatred is never overcome by more hatred. It is love that overcomes hatred. This is an eternal law.

"The third aspect of the Middle Path is Right Speech. The Buddha describes this as,

> Words that have four qualities are well-spoken, not ill spoken; faultless, not blamed by the wise. One speaks words that are beautiful, not ugly; one speaks words that are right, not wrong; one speaks words that are kind, not cruel; one speaks words that are truthful, not false.

"Also, we should say,

> I will speak at the right time, not at the wrong time. I will speak about what is, not what is not; I will speak with gentleness, not harshness; I will speak about the good, not about what is not good; I will speak with a mind filled with love, not with a mind filled with ill-will."[6]

"That means, Bhante, that our speech must promote peace, truth, and harmony," added Diana.

"Yes, you are correct. Before we speak we must consider and be mindful of the five conditions, which I will explain now. They are:

> Do I speak the truth?
> Do I speak gently?
> Do my words benefit others?
> Do I speak out of goodwill?
> Do I speak at the proper time and place?[7]

"Diana, do you have any questions about what I have explained so far?"

"No, Bhante, it is clear, and I understand. Please continue," she requested.

"The fourth aspect of the Middle Path is Right Action, which implies respect for life, property, and personal relationships. That means that one should avoid killing, stealing, and sexual misconduct. In regard to killing, I cite the Buddha's words in the Dhammapada, verse 129:

> All tremble at violence; all fear death. Putting oneself in the place of others, kill none, nor have them killed.

"Stealing from others reinforces latent greed, craving, and lying in the person who steals. It also causes sorrow to the victim. Every person has the right to keep the things he owns. The Buddha said, 'He who takes nothing that is not given, I call him virtuous and wise.' Refraining from sexual misconduct demonstrates self-respect. The Buddha said that one who indulges in sexual misconduct creates problems and suffering for himself as well as others; he also puts himself in danger of losing his reputation and making enemies.

"The next aspect is Right Livelihood, which means that one's way of living should not be harmful to others and should show respect for the life and goodwill of all living beings. There are five kinds of livelihood considered unwholesome, because they lead to suffering and unhappiness in society. These five are:

> Trade in deadly weapons
> Trade in animals for slaughter
> Trade in slavery
> Trade in intoxicants
> Trade in poisons

"The sixth aspect is Right Effort, which requires the development of the following four kinds of effort:

There is the effort to prevent *unwholesome*
    thoughts from arising in the mind, such as the
    desire for the property of others.
There is the effort to remove *unwholesome*
    thoughts that have already arisen in one's
    mind.
There is the effort to cultivate *wholesome*
    thoughts of love and compassion.
There is the effort to maintain the *wholesome*
    thoughts that have already arisen in the mind.

"The seventh aspect is Right Mindfulness, which is an essential quality in our daily activities. It is the constant awareness of our deeds, words, and thoughts. We should be completely aware and mindful of everything we do, whether it is sitting, standing, walking, or lying down. The Buddha said,

It is always good
    For the mindful one.
The mindful one
    Thrives in happiness.
Each day
    It is better
For the mindful one,
    The wakeful one.[8]

"The final practice of the Middle Path is Right Concentration, which is cultivated by the practice of meditation. Meditation is directed toward the development of awareness, intuition, sensitivity, and compassion. One of its by-products is a healthy state of being, both mental and physical.

"When we come into this world we inherit the mental characteristics of our previous lives, which were formed over the period of many life cycles. These characteristics often become habits, which are not easy to change. As a result, we accumulate many positive and negative karmic results in this life.

"Meditation helps to purify our minds. In addition, meditation cultivates concentration to help us achieve Right Understanding. Furthermore, it helps us to release our tensions and anxieties in positive directions.

"The Noble Eightfold Path that I have just explained is called the Middle Path, and according to the Buddha, any individual who follows this path is destined to find contentment, fulfillment, and happiness."

Diana had a wonderful, peaceful glow about her person. I was delighted to see her so happy. She said joyfully, "Bhante, I understand. I am enlightened!"

Then, very calmly, I asked her to explain to me in a few sentences what she understood. I wanted to make sure that she had interpreted my words correctly.

Diana replied, "Bhante, I see where I can apply to my life what you have just explained. I almost decided to drop my history class, but now I won't. My professor was always mean to me, and that made me angry. Using the Four Noble Truths I realize that the problem, or 'suffering,' as you call it, is something I created. I am often tardy to my history class, which is the cause of the problem with my professor. If I attend class on time, my professor won't be unhappy with me, and I won't get angry at him. That would bring about the cessation of suffering and the end to my problem. Finally, I can see that when I overcome *all* of my self-created problems I will be *totally* free from *all* suffering. Isn't that cool?" Diana was obviously delighted with her newfound understanding, and she had used her own life's problems as her teachers, which made it all the more real for her.

"I am glad you so quickly understand the Buddha's words. I presume that in our mutual cycle of samsara that you have been both a Buddhist and an aquaintance of mine."

This incident at Northwestern occurred in early 1977.

In 1993 I went to the New York Buddhist Vihara in Queens. The International Vesak celebrations were to be held in downtown Manhattan on the following day, and much to my delight, Ven. Piyatissa and Ven. Kondanna invited me to join them for this event.

When we arrived at the site of the celebration, we were seated in the front row of folding chairs, and our names were sent to the chairperson so we could be acknowledged as visiting monks. I noticed the chairperson glancing at me a few times, but I paid her no heed. She introduced the monks and explained how she had become a Buddhist.

"It was during a period of studies at Northwestern University that a saffron-robed Buddhist monk made an indelible impression on my life. This monk had a happy, serene countenance. He was always calm—even at the height of exams when the other students were running amok. He introduced me to Buddhism. That monk, Bhante Walpola Piyananda, is with us today. I welcome you, venerable sir, to our celebration. It is sixteen years since I last saw you, and during that period I have been studying and practicing the great religion you introduced me to. Thank you, Bhante."

After her introduction, she asked me to deliver a talk on Buddhism. It was an emotional moment for me, especially since I had come unprepared to speak. I humbly walked up to the podium as I recalled my first meeting with Diana. I was happy that she had continued studying the Noble Path of the Buddha, and I was delighted to see her as the president of the New York Buddhist Association.

I delivered a spontaneous speech on karma, as I firmly believed that my karmic ties with Diana were being renewed on that day. The following is a summary of my talk.

Karma means action, our mental, verbal, and bodily behavior. It is an intentional action that is performed deliberately, and every action produces a certain reaction. Actions are considered wholesome if they produce happiness for oneself and others, and unwholesome if they produce suffering. This is the law of cause and effect. The effect of one's past karma determines to some extent the nature of one's present situation in life.

The Buddha said, "According to the seed that is sown, so is the fruit that you reap. The doer of goodwill gathers good results. The doer of evil reaps evil results. If you plant a good seed well, then you will enjoy the good fruits."[9]

In Buddhism, every individual is an architect of his own destiny. What we enjoy today is the combined result of our actions in the past, present, and even in our previous lives through karmic force. This force has been compared to an electric current. A light bulb wears out, but the electrical current will brighten a new bulb when it is replaced. It is the same when a person dies and karma moves the life force from one body to the next.

This process goes through a series of births and deaths until both positive and negative karmas are completely eradicated. Then there is no craving, attachment, or rebirth. What is left is the ultimate bliss of *nibbana*.[10]

Here, I wish to quote the words of the Buddha again: "All beings are the owners of their actions, the heirs of their actions. Their actions are the womb from which they spring; with their actions they are bound up; their actions are their refuge. Whatever actions they do, good or bad, they will inherit those actions."[11]

It was sixteen years ago, at Northwestern University, that I planted a seed of Buddhism in the mind of an individual who, I believe, certainly had Buddhist ties in her previous lives. I am sure that Diana will continue her Buddhist work to the best of her ability. I wish her success, and may the Triple Gem guide her in this task.

After the Vesak celebration the other monks and I returned to the Vihara and had a serious discussion about how we as Buddhist *sangha* members can create a valuable impression on any society in which we live. As Bhante Piyatissa said that evening, "It is not only through our words and actions, but also through our maintenance of composed, contented, serene appearances, that we radiate the essence of our purified way of life. In this way we can attract others to follow the Path of the Buddha."

> When a traveler at last comes home
> From a far journey,
> With what gladness
> His family and his friends receive him!
> Even so shall your good deeds
> Welcome you like friends,
> And with what rejoicing
> When you pass from this life to the
>   next![12]

NINE

Detachment—A Way of Life

A group of Buddhists in rural Wisconsin organized a spiritual retreat, and they invited me to teach meditation. I was also asked to provide personal counseling on a one-on-one rotation basis while the others meditated.

My first counseling session was with Mary, a very frustrated young woman who was pregnant with her second child. She was married to Mario, an Italian national who had been living in the United States for five years. He was the father of her eldest child and also of the one who was due in about two months.

Mary told me that even though she loved Mario, he was irresponsible; he had no desire to work and provide for her and the children, and he was a constant partygoer who always returned home late. She said that she couldn't understand why Mario was this way because he was always telling her, "I am a Buddhist, and I practice detachment." This caused Mary to be confused about Buddhism and even more frustrated with Mario.

After hearing Mary's side of the story I said to her,

"Mario's interpretation of Buddhist teaching is not exactly correct in its essence, but before I say anything further I think I had better speak with him directly."

So, my second session was with Mario, who came to me reluctantly, because Mary had insisted. Mario was a handsome, rugged sort of man who seemed to not have a care in the world.

"Mario, please be seated," I said to him. He gave me a big smile and sat down. It was obvious to me that he was relaxed in my presence.

"Bhante, I have a feeling that you are psychic. I think you know a lot about me even though we just met. Is this true?"

"Mario, we are not here to talk about me or my psychic ability. We are here to talk about *you*. Please tell me what your plans are?"

I could tell that my reply caught him off guard. I could also tell that Mario was used to being charming and having the upper hand in conversation.

"Bhante," he began, "I am like a bird. I am a free man, and within two weeks I'll be leaving for Europe."

"How can you do that? Your wife is expecting a baby soon."

"But Bhante, I didn't want any children."

"You should take care of her and not abandon her and your children, is this not true?"

"Bhante, you sound like a Catholic priest."

"Of course, Mario," I responded. "All priests, regardless of their religion, will give the same advice not to shirk paternal responsibilities."

Mario looked at me defensively and said, "I have read Herman Hesse's book *Siddhartha* fourteen times. I can even recite many parts of it from memory. I am following Siddhartha's way of life. I do not have attachment to anything, not even to my own child. I am following the teaching of 'Buddhist detachment.' So wherever I wish to go, I go.

Wherever I want to sleep, I sleep. I lead a very easygoing life."

"Mario, the book *Siddhartha*, which is your bible, is not a Buddhist book. It is a beautifully written novel, which has touched the hearts and minds of many readers. It has also caused a number of readers to become curious about Buddhism. But Mario, Herman Hesse was not a practicing Buddhist, or even a Buddhist scholar. In fact, Hesse was a German novelist and philosopher who merely had very romantic notions about the nature of Buddhism. In addition, you should be careful about using the term *detachment* in the Buddhist sense, because I am quite positive that you do not understand what it means."

"Bhante, what are you talking about? Siddhartha himself abandoned his wife and son and left the palace—even without permission from his parents. He was the heir to the kingdom; what do I have to lose?"

"Mario, Siddhartha never abandoned his wife and child. He asked his parents for permission and left with parental blessings."

"That is not what I read," he replied with emotion. "It completely contradicts your statement."

"Mario, have you read the early Buddhist canon, which was recorded before the fourth century BCE?"

"I have not, Bhante." I could see that Mario was beginning to become a bit uncomfortable.

I continued with, "In the Middle-Length Discourses of the Buddha,[1] 'The Noble Search,' and 'The Greater Discourse to the Saccaka,'[2] it is explicitly mentioned that Prince Siddhartha left the palace *with* his parents' permission. Furthermore, in Lalitavistara, a Sanskrit text from the first century BCE, it says, 'My son, your desire for the emancipation of the world is worthy of encouragement as it will be beneficial for all mankind. May your wish be fulfilled.'[3] According to the early texts, the Prince *never* abandoned his wife. He provided for all of her needs, and for luxuries as well, and with her permission, he left the palace to pursue his enlightenment.

"I'll also tell you this, Mario. There was a well-known Buddhist commentator who lived in the fourth century CE, named Buddhaghosa. It was he who misconstrued the facts and added the abandonment myth to give the story a poetic, or even somewhat dramatic, effect. Also, I would like you to read *Old Path, White Clouds* by Thich Nhat Hanh. He, too, through his investigation of the early texts, supports the fact that Prince Siddhartha left his wife and family *with* permission."[4]

"Bhante, I suppose you are right, but you are talking about the Theravada interpretation. I am following Zen practice, which is Mahayana. Therefore *my* detachment is *Zen* detachment."

"Mario, just so you are informed, Thich Nhat Hanh is a Mahayana Zen master. Also, you are not the only Westerner who calls himself a Buddhist who only understands the *literal* definitions of attachment and detachment. The fact that you practice Zen meditation has nothing to do with your understanding of this very important Buddhist theme." I could tell that Mario was on the verge of getting angry with me, particularly because I wasn't impressed by his Zen practice, or by his reading of Herman Hesse.

I paused for a moment before I continued, and I thought of an anecdote that I felt was appropriate. "Mario," I began, "I would like to tell you a story about a man named Ted who was constantly changing his girlfriends. When I questioned him about this, he replied unabashed, 'I practice nonattachment. If I stick to one person, I will become attached to her. This I have learned from my master.'

"I replied to Ted that I believed he had misunderstood his master. I also told him that it seemed he was attached to his nonattachment, much the way I think you are, Mario.

When a person is in love with another person, then he or she has to accept the responsibilities that go along with that love. Otherwise, it is not love at all, but merely an impersonal lust. Love is a state of unity, which is experienced physically as well as mentally. With love, there is caring, forgiveness, and commitment. Buddhism teaches that love unites, whereas *your* theory of detachment results in fragmentation."

Mario replied, "Getting back to Ted, I think he is right, Bhante."

"Mario, I believe you were born a Catholic."

"In Italy nearly everyone is a Catholic, Bhante, and for a number of years I even studied in a seminary to become a Catholic priest."

I was very surprised to hear this, but I responded, "That's good, Mario. Do you remember Luke fourteen, verse thirty-six? It says, 'If anyone comes to me and does not hate his own father and mother and wife and children, and brothers and sisters, yes, and even his own life, he cannot be my disciple.'[5] What Jesus meant here was not literally to hate your family and yourself, but to renounce the world. If you take this passage literally, you would hate your family and yourself. But what he meant here was to renounce."

"I see your point, Bhante."

"Even the Buddhist Dhammapada has a story very similar to the Christian one, and I'll share it with you. One day when the Buddha was in his Jetavana monastery, he saw a monk named Bhaddiya coming toward him. The Buddha remarked, '*Bhikkhus,* look at that monk. He has killed both his father and his mother and he goes about without feeling any remorse.' The Bhikkhus could not understand this statement because that particular monk had committed no crime.

"Then the Buddha explained that he was referring to an Arahat, who has eradicated craving, conceit, wrong beliefs, and attachment to the sense bases and the objects of the senses. The Buddha had made this statement using metaphors. The terms *mother* and *father* are meant to be *craving* and *conceit*."[6]

"Oh, Bhante, that's too heavy for me. I don't understand."

"Let me explain an experience I once had. Several years ago when I was preparing to leave the temple for a funeral service, John, a meditation practitioner, came rushing toward me, pleading with me to listen to him. I told him to talk to the visiting Zen meditation master, as I was already late. I returned after two hours to find John still waiting for me. He was visibly upset and told me that the meditation master had agreed with him when he expressed his desire to end his own life. I told John that I didn't believe this was true, because the first principle of monkhood is to never encourage anyone to take a life, including one's own. I knew that John must have misunderstood, and I asked him to please explain exactly what had happened.

"John answered, 'Bhante, I was so depressed that I wanted to kill myself, and I told the Zen master of my intention. After a long pause, the monk said to me, 'You kill yourself.' I was shocked, Bhante, and I said to him, 'I beg your pardon?' Again the monk repeated, 'You kill yourself. You kill yourself.'

"Mario, if you were in my position, what advice would *you* have given John?"

Mario replied with a grin, "I would tell John to file a complaint at the police station against the Zen master."

"Mario, let me explain. When the monk told John to kill himself, he meant that he should kill his 'self,' or his ego, not end his life or do harm to his body. Mario, you are faced with the same problem. You are using the word *nonattachment* as a shroud to cover your weaknesses and to run away from your responsibilities. You have to take care of Mary. You are legally married and you have children with her. She is your wife. Please understand that a successful relationship depends on three important elements: the first is *metta*, or loving kindness; the second is *pema*, or personal affection; and the third is *raga*, or sexual attraction.

"Loving kindness means having compassion for all human beings. Personal affection means to have feelings of respect, love, and emotional attachment for your parents, siblings, and also for your wife and your children. Sexual attraction is a desire that is aroused in an individual and leads to satisfying his or her basic physical needs. Mario, it seems that you have sixty percent sexual attraction, thirty percent loving kindness, and only ten percent personal affection."

"Bhante, you have given me much food for thought. Could you help me find a way to live a happy medium and still be detached?"

"As I mentioned earlier, your theory of detachment is completely incorrect. You are attached to that incorrect view. You should be able to face challenges, not run away from them. When you live with another person, regardless of your marital status, you are responsible for doing your best to promote each other's happiness. You should help each other maintain a happy, well-balanced life. By practicing consideration you will be able to make Mary happy. If she is not happy, how can you or the children be happy? The root cause of family strife is lack of communication and understanding. Have you spoken to Mary about your European vacation?"

"Yes, Bhante; she is furious with me, and she argues about it day and night. I am sick of it. She wants to make me feel guilty because she is pregnant. She wants child support for my son, but she doesn't want the two-year-old to join me on my holiday."

"Mario, our Lord Buddha has advised all husbands to honor, respect, and be faithful to their wives. They should love, be attentive, provide for the basic needs, and take care of the children."[7]

"I think the mother must also share this burden," he replied.

"Yes, both parents have to share this responsibility. A mother's duty is to love, care for, and protect the children. Parents are responsible for the well-being and upbringing of their children. The father should be the son's role model."

I continued, "Do you know that many Sri Lankans have immigrated to the United States mainly to educate their children? These people, whom I know personally, lived very comfortable lives in Sri Lanka and did not lack anything. Yet, for their children's education they have sacrificed their lives of luxury to live in America. They do not lead an easy life here, and with great difficulty, they support the children until their education is completed. Most Sri Lankan students do not work while studying. The children of these Sri Lankans are very fortunate to have such dedicated and sacrificing parents. The children appreciate the hardships the parents endure, and they often become successful figures in this society."

"Bhante, I should follow the Sri Lankan tradition. On second thought, I may not go to Europe. I want to invite you to my house before you leave. I am being attached to you now."

I was relieved to hear Mario's decision, and I was happy that I had been able to lead Mario to understand his personal responsibilities and to redefine his understanding of Buddhist detachment.

A short verse from the Dhammapada sums it up nicely:

> Why do now what you will regret
>   later?
> Why bring future tears upon yourself?
> Do only what you are sure you will not
>   regret
> And you will always be filled with joy.[8]

TEN

A Lady of the Night

I arrived in the United States on July 4, 1976, the two-hundredth anniversary of America's birth. The country's determination to hold on to its old image of power, might, and right had collapsed under its own weight, and by 1976 these notions had disappeared within the pain of the Vietnam War. Nothing seemed sure any more. Despite the hopeful exterior, a crack had become noticeably apparent in the center of the collective American mind. In reality, most Americans found it hard to find any hope in this bicentennial celebration. Fear for America's future was hiding beneath the surface of the American dream.

These polarities of hope and fear seemed to display themselves in subtle ways. Yet it is the openness between polarities that allows for the flow of the river, and such openness has been one of the transforming qualities that attracts new followers to Buddhism. I was, in many ways and to many people, a symbol of the potential for change and openness, while at the same time I was feared as an unknown entity. I was everything and nothing at the same time. Buddhism, to those who were searching, became a symbol of possibility: an open locus of no dimension, the openness between the disjunctive pairs of hope and fear, the middle path, a potentiality for something as new as the vision of America's forefathers. This was the secret dream. Some Americans seemed to be looking for fresh directions distinct from the vacuous materialism they had come to despise. Nineteen seventy-six. Red, white, and very blue.

On Wednesday and Friday evenings I taught meditation at the International Buddhist Meditation Center in Los Angeles, where I had come to live. At that time I was the only Theravada monk in the area who worked with Westerners. Most other Theravada monks were Thai, working within their own community, and primarily with first-generation immigrants.

One Wednesday evening before class, a lady came up to me and offered me an envelope. I thanked her and placed it beside me as we began our session. At the end of our meditation she came over and urged me to open the envelope. I had seen the woman a few times before, but she had always left very soon after meditation ended. I didn't know anything about her except that her name was Kathy.

"Bhante," she said, "Don't you want to open your gift, the envelope?" She pointed to it. "Go ahead and open it!"

I thanked her and replied that in my country we usually do not open gifts in front of the giver. Kathy again insisted with the delightfulness of a child that I open the envelope. Reluctantly, I agreed.

"Oh my gosh!" I said. I could hardly believe my eyes! I looked again and sure enough there were three one-hundred-dollar bills. This was more than I had ever received before, an amount considered a lot of money in my country of Sri Lanka, where even top executives didn't make three hundred dollars in a month.

I looked up from the envelope and responded, "My, this

is quite a nice gift! Thank you so much for your wonderful thoughtfulness. You must have a very good position, my friend. Tell me, what do you do for a living?"

She looked a bit uncomfortable, but she replied, "Bhante, you see, I am a hooker. . . ."

Certainly I did not have the foggiest idea what a *hooker* was, but I thought to myself that such a large amount of money must mean that she held a very good job.

I said, "Oh, what a wonderful career. You must be very happy."

Her face drew a puzzled look. Suddenly, like a dam breaking, she smiled and exclaimed, "Oh, Bhante, thank you! Everyone always puts me down, but you praise me. Thank you!"

Almost instantly her happiness suddenly vanished, and instead she was crying. "Oh, Bhante," she sniffed, "they wouldn't even let me go to my mother's memorial service! I was kicked out because they had called me a shameful person. Bhante, thank you for being so kind and accepting. Not one person has ever accepted me for myself."

I wasn't sure just what was going on, so I thanked her again and asked if she would please come back for Friday's meditation. She agreed and left like a flash, as if she wished to completely disappear. I feared I had somehow embarrassed her.

As soon as she was gone, I immediately jumped up and ran into the office. "Mike, Mike," I yelled. "Come quick, come here."

Mike came running into the room. "Are you OK, Bhante?" he asked.

"Yes, yes, I am fine. But I must ask you a question," I responded.

"Well, what is so urgent? I've never seen you in such a hurry," Mike replied with curiosity.

"Mike," I proceeded, "I need you to tell me what a *hooker* is!"

Mike's look of astonishment, combined with his gasping for air, made me panic for a moment. With a start he replied, "What? You don't need to know what that is! Why do you ask? You don't need to know that. I am not going to discuss it." Mike began to huff out of the room.

I grabbed his arm softly. "Mike, please. I need to know. I don't understand, but I asked one of our meditators what she did for a living. She had given me a large donation, and I was shocked at the size of it. So I asked her what was her career. When she told me she was a hooker, I praised her. Then she started crying, saying everyone puts her down except me."

Mike's face was as white as a cloud, and suddenly he burst into laughter, like a spring shower. "You're kidding me, aren't you Bhante?"

I wasn't, and I guess Mike could tell by the look on my face.

"Bhante, just a minute. I'll be back in a minute." With that, Mike left the room. I was still confused when a few moments later he returned with the abbot of the center and a few giggling others.

"Bhante, please sit down," the abbot requested, pointing to the chair. I slowly moved over, wondering what I had gotten myself into.

"Bhante, I heard your story from Mike. You really don't need to know what a *hooker* is, but in this case"—the abbot stopped speaking suddenly while the people in the hallway moved by—"in this case, obviously you need to know. A hooker is a harlot, a streetwalker . . . a . . . a prostitute!"

I was astounded. I certainly knew what a prostitute was, but I was not up on all the new American slang. But there was the realization: Kathy—a prostitute. I felt so bad, and I wondered what might have happened in her life to bring her into such a livelihood. I thanked the abbot for his information and left for my quarters.

All night long I could not sleep. I worried for Kathy's well-being. I wondered if I should have accepted the money that she had earned in such a way. I tossed and turned and got up and meditated, but I could not sleep. What was I going to do? How might I be of service to her without being judgmental?

Then it came to my mind that the Lord Buddha worked with prostitutes, and he understood them. Sirima and Ambapali were prostitutes who eventually became two of Buddha's greatest supporters. I should try to understand what happened, how Kathy had come to this kind of life. I decided that I would speak to her about it and hoped that she would be at Friday's meditation, as she said she would be. She was.

When Kathy sat down I quietly asked her if she could see me after meditation. I could tell by the look on her face that she was wondering if I was going to condemn her. I just smiled and struck the bell to start our session.

Afterward, Kathy and I went into the Shrine Room. There, a large, beautiful, golden Buddha sat quietly in repose, next to where we settled. I gazed over at the image for inspiration and support.

Turning to her, I said, "Tell me, why are you leading this kind of life? I want to ask you . . ."

At this point Kathy interrupted me and blurted out, "I knew it! You're going to put me down, too! Everyone puts me down."

I stopped her with a look. "No. No. No. I am being compassionate. I am not judging you. I am also worried about your welfare."

She stopped for a second and looked at me. "Bhante," she said, "no one has ever cared for me except my dear mother, who is now dead. Could it be that someone I just met would care for me? Why? Why?" She sobbed on and on.

"My friend, please. When I am of service to you, I am of

service to the Lord Buddha. You and the Buddha have the same nature. Please tell me, how is it that you came to this way of life? Please tell me about yourself. I will not harm you; I only wish to help you."

She looked so alone and scared. I continued, "Kathy, in the Buddha's time there were so many women who were prostitutes, but later became wonderful ladies; they became faithful supporters of the Lord Buddha, and some of them even became Buddhist nuns!"

A light seemed to dawn on her face.

"Oh, Bhante, my father left when I was very young; my mother was frightened and married the first man that came along. My stepfather was a wild man. He abused and kicked her, put her down, and beat me, too." Kathy continued, "While I was in high school I fell in love with a man who took advantage of me, and after I became pregnant he left me and I didn't know what to do. My mom was a Catholic, and she wanted me to have the child. Mom helped, but I had to drop out of school. I applied for welfare and was rejected."

Kathy was beginning to tremble. I looked toward her to reassure her. "Please continue, friend," I said.

"There was so much trouble with Mom's boyfriend. He stole money and continued to beat us both! Finally Mom left the guy. Then another man came into my life, and he also began to abuse me. Meanwhile, my mother had a stroke. I couldn't afford to care for her, and I had no money to care for my child. I wanted to commit suicide, but the thought of my child prevented me."

She began again to weep, fixing her gaze into infinite space.

"Kathy," I spoke softly. "My friend, you have been hurt so many times. I hope to be one of many that will come forth to help you as you walk down a new path. You have a child who can love you and bring comfort and happiness. I can tell you a story about a woman who suffered great tragedy. You will see that even with her losses she was able to overcome her sorrows and misfortunes through the guidance of the Buddha. I would like you to listen carefully to this story about Patacara.

"She was the daughter of a wealthy banker and was brought up in a home of luxury and love. When Patacara was a teenager, she fell in love with a handsome male servant in her family's household. She knew that her father would never accept their relationship, so she ran away with her lover and together they lived in a small village far from her childhood home. Her father disowned her and said he never wanted to see her again. She desperately wanted to visit her parents' house when she was expecting her first child, but her lover was afraid that Patacara's father would turn them away. She decided to go anyway, but the child was born during the early part of the journey, and they were forced to turn back to their village. When she became pregnant with her second child she was determined that it would be born in her parents' home. Midway through the journey she started to go into labor, but a fierce storm had started to brew. Her lover left her to collect wood and branches so as to build a shelter to protect Patacara and the child that would be born, but a snake bit him and he died. Patacara gave birth and, grieving, decided she had no choice but to continue her journey to her parents' home. Eventually she came to the point where she had to cross a flooded river called Accirawati.

"When she came near the bank of the river she thought, I am very weak because last night I birthed a child, lost a great deal of blood, and have had no food or sleep. I cannot carry both children at the same time. So she left the older boy on the riverbank while she carried the newly born infant across the raging torrent. When she reached the other side, she broke off some leafy branches of a tree and spread them on the ground. Then she put the young child on them and returned to cross the river for the older one.

"She had hardly gotten to midstream when a hawk saw the baby child and, considering him food, swooped down from the sky to grab him. The mother, seeing the hawk about to take away the child, screamed with a loud voice, '*Su! Su!*'

"The older boy, hearing his mother's voice, thought she was calling him. So he hurriedly jumped into the water, even though he couldn't swim. Seeing this, the mother frantically tried to reach him, but the swift current swept him away, even while the hawk carried off her new baby.

"Now, Patacara was very, very sad. She wailed and cried, saying, 'One of my sons has been carried off by a hawk; the other has been swept away by the water; by the roadside my husband lies dead of snakebite.'

"She went off in the direction of her family's village, crying all the way. Eventually she met a man on the road and asked him, 'Sir, where do you live?'

"'In Savatthi,' he answered.

"She described a particular family in a particular location in the city of Savatthi. 'Do you know them, sir?' she asked.

"'Yes, lady, I know them,' he replied, 'but don't ask me about that family. Ask me about any other family you know, and I will tell you about them.'

"'Oh, sir, I know only that family. Please tell me about them,' she replied.

"'Since you insist, I cannot hide the truth,' said the man. 'Did you know that there was a big storm and heavy rain last night?' he asked her.

"'Yes,' answered the lady, 'I know. It rained only on me, I suppose, because I had the worst of it.'

"'In that heavy rain,' continued the man, 'that house you are asking about was destroyed. Its walls fell in on the father, mother, and only son.'

"'Oh no! Don't tell me they are dead, too!' said the lady.

"'Yes. Can you see that fire over there?' he asked, pointing to some flames a short distance away. 'That is their funeral pyre,' said the man with sadness.

"Then the woman completely lost her mind. She roamed the streets without any clothes. The people thought she was crazy, and wherever she went, they drove her away. Finally, one day, she arrived in Jetavana, where the Buddha was preaching. As she approached the Buddha, a man threw a robe over her. The Buddha, hearing her story, spoke to her compassionately and gave her hope to continue her life. He explained that life is a challenge and that we cannot run away from our problems; we have to face them and overcome them as well.

"In spite of all of these adversities, Patacara was able to survive and eventually to grow spiritually to become an enlightened nun. She later became a great teacher and many women stricken with grief sought her guidance.[1]

"Kathy, you have a lesson to learn from Patacara. My friend, the Buddha spoke numerous times about the connection between poverty and corruption. He clearly stated that poverty is the cause of immorality and crimes such as theft, falsehood, violence, hatred, and cruelty. Kings in ancient times made the mistake of trying to suppress crime with punishment, but to no avail. Even today our modern governments act out of this ignorance. With the building of so many new prisons and the lack of funds for education, they still try to suppress crime through punishment; again to no avail. Even so many centuries ago the Buddha explained the futility of such a policy.

"The Buddha suggested that in order to rid society of crime, the economic condition of the people should be improved. He went into detail and explained that capital should be provided for business and traders, grain and machines for farmers, and adequate wages for all workers. No

wonder we have problems! The Buddha told us that livelihood should come from efforts that are not harmful to
one's self or to others and that when communities are sus-
tained in this way, the world will be free from crime and become peaceful.[2]

"Furthermore, the Lord Buddha expressed that there are
four kinds of effort that we must apply to organizing our lives.
These four kinds of effort, or *Satara Sampaphadana*, are:[3]

Prevention (*Sanvara*). This means preventing unwholesome thoughts from arising in the mind, as these thoughts
will give rise to unwholesome actions. *Sanvara* also means
that you should be mindful of your own protection in order
to safeguard your life.

Removal (*Pahana*). This is the removal of unwholesome
thoughts that have already arisen in your mind. When a person has had bad experiences, he or she tends to harbor them
deep inside and often refuses to let go of these bad feelings.
People who suffer are those who hang on to grudges and
negative feelings toward others. You can remove such unhealthy thoughts by practicing loving kindness.

Cultivation (*Bhavana*). You must always maintain wholesome and positive thoughts in your mind. You can do this
by having a goal in your life. You should also be skilled, efficient, earnest, and energetic in whatever worthwhile activity you are engaged. You should protect the income that you
earn righteously. You should have good friends, who are
faithful, learned, virtuous, and intelligent, friends who will
guide you on the right path. You should live according to
your means and lead a balanced life.

Maintenance (*Anurakhana*). You have been born into a
society that theoretically practices and values high ethics.
Human beings have evolved highly developed and discern-
ing minds. With those minds we should be able to differentiate what is useful and beneficial from what is useless and

harmful. *Anurakhana,* therefore, means that we should keep and maintain the useful and beneficial and make sure that it continues to grow and expand in our minds. By the same token, we should discard the useless and harmful as soon as we discover it. Maintenance of useful and beneficial attributes will help us as individuals, and will help the society in which we live.

"Finally, Kathy, try not to burden yourself with an unhealthy guilty conscience. Human nature is such that no one is all good and no one is all bad; the same goes for you. Even if you have done something wrong, you don't have to forever feel guilty about it. Instead, you should take advantage of the opportunity to correct yourself and make long-lasting and positive changes. You should also not waste time by feeling remorse about your past. Kathy, I want you to wake up and declare to yourself that it is a new day and that you have twenty-four precious hours ahead of you. Please think of spending each of those hours looking for ways to bring happiness to yourself, as well as to others.

"Kathy, are you interested in finding a new way of life? A first step in this direction might be creating a new way to establish right livelihood. That means work that does not harm you or harm others. Would you like to hear about a training program I know about?" I asked respectfully.

"Yes, of course!" she responded eagerly.

"Well, a friend of mine, Ana, has studied with an organization called Jobs for Progress to learn new job skills. Her teacher's name is Claudia. Here is her phone number. I will contact Ana and Claudia today to let them know that you will be calling. OK?"

"Great!" Kathy exclaimed, and a broad smile of freedom arose on her face.

Kathy's look reminded me of Patacara, the one who had surmounted the stormy seas of tragedy and not only lived to tell about it, but attained enlightenment as well. The river Kathy faced was gently flowing now. The painful emotions she had felt began to fade like the moon in the morning sky. As we sat talking in the Shrine Room, she radiated fresh belief, belief born anew, belief that she could and would find a new way of life. Such belief had risen in her heart, displacing the darkness that had so long ruled there. Her own happiness in the face of blind hope, along with her desperate fear, had seen her to a new shore.

As a postscript, Kathy followed up with Ana and Claudia and eventually became a case worker in the Los Angeles County Human Resources Department, where she works tirelessly to this day for the protection of abused children.

> So wake, reflect, watch.
> Work with care and attention.
> Live in the Way,
> And the light will grow in you.[4]

ELEVEN

Fidelity and Faith

I have been a spiritual adviser to the Southeast Asian Buddhist community in Los Angeles for the past two decades. Among the Asian communities, it has been my experience that the Laotians and the Cambodians have had the most difficult time adjusting to their new society. Unfortunately, most of the adults have a limited knowledge of the English language and oftentimes find it hard to obtain suitable employment. This is the common starting point for their problems.

Since I was closely associating with the Laotian and Cambodian people, it was natural that I eventually assumed the role of personal adviser and confidant to many of the individuals within these communities.

One day Sovi and his wife, Mimi, visited me at my temple. They were immigrants from Laos, and they had a personal problem to discuss. I invited them into my office for privacy.

Sovi, in an extremely angry manner, began ranting about his unfaithful wife. The couple had three children and they had been married for almost sixteen years. Mimi, however, had become dissatisfied with her husband and had gone out seeking greener pastures. She eventually began to neglect her household responsibilities as a wife and a mother. She began to go out every night and return home very late, always claiming a plausible excuse. The children were beginning to dislike her and had lost respect for her, since they suspected she was being unfaithful to their father.

"Sovi, was she like this during the early years of your marriage?" I asked, trying to redirect the tone of the meeting.

"No Bhante, she was a devoted wife and a caring mother who attended to all the children's needs. She was a responsible housewife and always awaited my arrival home from work with a cheerful smile. This past year she has totally changed her behavior, and her mother believes that she is possessed by an evil spirit."

Mimi was silent, never even looking up while Sovi was speaking. I asked Mimi if she would like to talk with me in private since I could tell she wouldn't speak in front of her angry husband. She told me she was willing, so I asked Sovi to wait in the Shrine Room while I talked to Mimi.

Mimi tearfully began telling me her side of the story. "My husband has become domineering, but my new boyfriend is kind, gentle, and understanding. I really love him. I want to move in with him, as I know he will take care of my needs."

"Mimi, don't you think that Sovi is a caring husband who loves your children?"

"Yes."

"Is he an alcoholic or a gambler?"

"No."

"Is he a womanizer?"

"No."

"Is he faithful to you?"

"Yes, Bhante. I know he loves me very much. Sometimes his constant endearing remarks irritate me. I feel I need to have my space."

"Mimi, has Sovi physically abused you?"

"Never, he has never touched me in anger."

I continued questioning her. "Does he embarrass you in front of the children?"

"No, he never does that."

"Does he have a problem with his in-laws?"

"No, Bhante, my parents adore him. At times I even feel jealous!"

"Mimi, according to your answers, your husband is a good man."

Mimi answered, "He used to be a good man. But recently he has changed and has started drinking."

"Maybe he has found out about your new boyfriend and wants to drown his sorrow. It is not a good way to cope, but maybe the poor man simply doesn't know how to deal with his emotions. Mimi, do you think Sovi will allow you to take his children with you when you leave him?" I asked.

"No, he will not," she replied sadly.

"Are you going away and leaving your children behind?"

"Yes, I love Roberto very much."

Then I recalled an ancient saying, "When a woman is in love, Mimi, she is blind to everything except the one she loves. It is the same with a man."

It was difficult to get Mimi to come down to the real world, yet I decided to take her with me to the Shrine Room so I could explain the Five Precepts of Buddhism to her and Sovi together. I remembered the Parliament of World Religions in 1993, which I attended in Chicago. The group as a whole represented all the religions of the world, and they all agreed to adopt a set of global ethics, which wound up being four of the five precepts as taught by the Buddha 2,500 years ago.

I addressed Sovi and Mimi in a very serious voice. "As Buddhists, both of you have been obligated to follow the Five Precepts. If you were following these precepts you would not be facing the problems you are having now in your relationship. Observing the precepts helps an individual to maintain good conduct, which prevents one from committing unwholesome actions."

I continued. "The first precept, as you know, is to refrain from killing.[1] Observing this precept means not only avoiding the killing of human beings, but also any living creature. In observing the first precept one has to protect life. Furthermore, one cultivates loving kindness toward all living beings.

"The second precept is to refrain from taking what is not given. It also means having respect for the property of others. This precept is an injunction against any form of stealing or dishonest dealing.

"The third precept urges us to avoid sexual misconduct. That means any sexual behavior that harms either others or ourselves. Rape would be the most obvious example of this precept. Adultery would be another. The Buddha said that people who indulge in sexual misconduct create problems and suffering for themselves as well as others. In observing this precept, one controls one's sexual desires and is faithful to one's husband or wife.

"The fourth precept is to not lie. According to Buddhism, perfect speech is a very important aspect of ethical training. The Buddha said, 'Words that have four qualities are well spoken, not ill spoken, faultless, not blamed by the wise. One speaks words that are beautiful, not ugly; one speaks words that are right, not wrong; one speaks words that are kind, not cruel; and one speaks words that are truthful, not false.'

"The fifth and final precept is based on maintaining mental health. It is the cultivation of the mind for mental development. It advises us to refrain from taking intoxicants such as alcohol and drugs.[2]

"As a Buddhist, if you follow the Five Precepts you will be able to achieve peace and harmony and live a successful life. It will also help your children follow you as a role model."

After this discussion Sovi and Mimi departed with my blessings. I knew, however, that talking to Mimi was like pouring water over a duck's back. I knew the problem had not been solved.

A few days later, nearing midnight, I got a frantic call from Mimi. She cried, "Bhante, I am in trouble. I am calling from a rest area in San Bernardino. Sovi is kidnapping me and threatening to kill me. He is also threatening to kill my three children when he gets back to the city. Please take care of my kids."

I heard a shriek as Sovi grabbed the telephone from her.

He screamed, "Bhante, I am going to kill this dirty woman. I will kill my children and kill myself, too. I do not want my children to suffer any more than they have because of the shame their mother has brought to our family."

I knew I had to make a quick decision. I responded to his threat with compassion. "Sovi, please listen to me. You are going to make a lot of trouble for me if you don't stop. When you kill Mimi, of course you'll end up in jail. I will have to visit you regularly because I love you. It's too much work for me! I can help you solve your problem. Please return to Los Angeles and come directly to the temple. I will be waiting for you. Promise me that you will come here with Mimi now."

"Okay," he responded slowly, then quickly hung up.

I wasn't certain that he would keep his word, so I went to his house and returned to the temple with the three young children and their grandmother. I gave them shelter in the adjacent building and waited for Sovi's return.

It was in the wee hours of the morning that I heard the

doorbell. I hadn't been able to sleep, of course, and I was relieved. When I opened the front door I was shocked to see that Sovi had become nearly insane with rage. He was dragging Mimi behind him with one hand and was carrying a gun in the other.

I told them to follow me to the Shrine Room. They walked behind me silently, and then I told Sovi to put the gun on the ground. After he obliged, I questioned him about his uncontrollable anger. I said, "Calm down or there will be a tragedy here tonight."

"Bhante, this woman always comes home very late after work. I know she is up to no good. Tonight I went to her working place and waited in the parking lot until she came out. There she was, leaving the building hand in hand with another man. I aimed my gun at the bastard but he ran away. I grabbed Mimi and pushed her into my car and drove toward the desert, where I was going to kill her."

"Sovi, you are a good man," I replied reassuringly. "You are good-looking, and you have a well-paying, respected trade. You can have a beautiful woman if you want to. If your wife isn't faithful to you, then let her go. Keep your cool and start a new life."

My words appeased Sovi. He then wanted to know where his children were, because when he called home there was no answer. I told him that the children were with me within the temple premises.

When I finally got him calmed down, I took him to see his children. I made him leave his gun with me and allowed him to go home with his family.

Sovi called me two days later saying that he was moving out with his children; he had found a place closer to his job. A year later he visited me with his new wife and children. They all seemed to be happy.

Another year passed and Mimi came to see me. Her love, Roberto, had left her. He was already married when he was courting her and had eventually dumped her to return to his wife, who was living in his native land.

Mimi cried her heart out. She regretted that she hadn't followed my advice. She begged me to call Sovi to allow her to visit her children.

I obliged Mimi and called Sovi. At first he was furious. Later, however, when I explained his ethical and paternal obligations, he came around and agreed to my request.

I did not want to judge Mimi for what she had done in the past. I blessed her and told her that I hoped she would gain a better understanding of human nature and develop her self-respect. I admonished her to follow the Five Precepts of Buddhism from that day forward, and she gave me her word that she would do so.

> From lust arises grief,
> From lust arises fear.
> For him who is free from lust
> There is no grief, much less fear.[3]
>
> Like a monkey in the forest
> You jump from tree to tree,
> Never finding the fruit—
> From life to life,
> Never finding peace.[4]

TWELVE

Buddhist Prosperity

I lived with Reverend Muthima from South Africa in the Garrett Methodist Seminary's dormitory at Northwestern University. Reverend Muthima was a Baptist minister who was studying for his Ph.D. He became my close friend, since he lived in the room next to mine. He often advised me very seriously to convert to Christianity. He believed that if I didn't become a Christian, I would certainly go to hell. We often had friendly arguments about religions. I seldom questioned his beliefs, since I respected his philosophy even though I didn't believe it myself. Unfortunately, Reverend Muthima always expressed how much he despised my faith, and it seemed to me that his outlook was very narrow. He was completely unwilling to explore other religious beliefs, let alone have faith in them.

It is with humor that I recall how he tried to humiliate me in front of the students. I remember we were both teaching assistants in Dr. Perry's comparative religion class. Dr. Perry was absent that day and I was assigned to teach "The Noble Eightfold Path." After the lesson Reverend Muthima stood up and praised me. Then he added, "My brother Piyananda, I have a great regard for you, therefore I do not want you to go to hell."

"Why do you think I'll go to hell?" I responded, smiling.

"The Bible says, 'For God so loved the world that he gave his only begotten son, that whosoever believeth in him shall have ever lasting life.' The Bible says this, so please accept Christianity, as only the Christians can go to heaven."

I was amused at his remark. I took the opportunity to make him stop trying to convert me. "Reverend, you will go to heaven with the other good people. Even in heaven you will be arguing about the various theories of religion. Your arguments will be an obstacle to my meditation. Therefore, I prefer to go to hell. Then I will be of service to the suffering."

Since that incident, Reverend Muthima never attempted to make me a Christian again. Yet, he always seemed to gain pleasure by looking upon Buddhism as a pessimistic religion.

One day he told the class that Buddhism is a religion for people who have renounced the world. He also added that Buddhism emphasizes impermanence and suffering. He believed that Buddhist countries were poor because of this.

I remained silent because I knew I would get a chance to answer him.

The following week was my turn to conduct the lesson. I was well prepared to respond to Reverend Muthima.

I began my lesson. "Buddhism is neither a pessimistic nor an optimistic religion. It is a realistic religion. The Buddha preached about the way in which an individual could be successful in life. He wanted people to strive hard to become their best in life; he wanted them to acquire wealth, while at the same time stressing that it had to be acquired through lawful and just means. He did not advocate pessimism. In fact, he taught his close devotee Anatapindika, 'Householder, there are five merits of earning wealth.' Let me explain to you what these five merits are.

"First of all, a wealthy person can live a healthy, happy, and long life, fulfilling all his needs. He can provide for his parents, his wife and children, and all dependents.

"Second, he can make provisions for his friends and associates.

"Third, when money is earned in a righteous manner, he can ward off any calamity.

"Fourth, he can make religious offerings, as well as help and entertain his friends and relatives.

"Finally, he can help those religious teachers who have given up their worldly desires.[1]

"Thus did the Buddha explain how to spend money wisely. Furthermore, he said that to lead a happy, successful life one must be generous, whether rich or poor. It is not the wealth amassed by an individual, but the generosity that matters.

"The idle can never be rich. The Buddha explained that there are three types of people. The first is the type who does not strive and who lacks enthusiasm; he is compared by the Buddha to a blind person; he doesn't have enough money to fend for himself, and neither can he help others.

"The second is the type of person who spends all that he has inherited. He is selfish and thinks only about himself. Therefore, he does not think about life after death. Also in this second category are people who practice charity and help others, but neglect their family's welfare and don't lead full lives.

"The third type of person, however, is the one who strives hard to make a success of his life, and therefore reaps the best benefits. He is happy in this life and he will be happy in the next life as well.[2]

"In the *Vyaggapajja Sutta* the Buddha advised that there are four things that lead to happiness. First of all, one should be skilled, efficient, earnest, and devoted to his profession. Second, one should carefully protect what he has earned through his righteous efforts. Third, one should associate only with wise, virtuous friends. And fourth, one should spend wisely, and in proportion to his income, enabling him to live within his means.[3] Furthermore, the Buddha also advised women as to how to manage the household economy. He instructed them to be aware of household responsibilities and to manage the finances efficiently, always having enough of a nest egg for a rainy day.

"The Buddha never praised poverty. He has said, 'Poverty is an ordeal for a person who is living a household life.' Therefore, the Buddha's advice to householders was to try to earn wealth justly, to spend it in a proper way, and to live a useful life.

"Speaking about a merchant who wished to be successful in his business, the Buddha said, 'A salesman should know the quality of the goods he buys; he should also know their price, and the amount of profit he gains on their sale; he should be skilled in the art of buying and selling; he should be honest and trustworthy, so that wealthy persons would deposit their money in his care.[4]

"On another occasion, the Buddha said that a trader should be active in his businesses throughout the day. If he is inactive and lazy, he will not be successful.[5]

"Before the passing away of the Buddha, he visited the village Pataligama and addressed his devotees, saying that the truly virtuous person was vigilant and energetic, and thereby, he would be successful in his business. He could earn a great mass of wealth as a result.[6]

"In the *Sigalovada Sutta* the Buddha advised about how to use income. 'Divide the income into four parts. One portion should be spent for one's daily expenses. Two portions should be used for the progression of one's businesses. One part should be deposited carefully for future use in case of failure or emergency.'[7]

"The Buddha was not against earning wealth right-eously, however, he strongly advised people to not earn money the wrong way. The wrong ways he mentioned are by taking away life, by stealing, by cheating, and by producing and selling intoxicants or drugs. He also forbade making and selling poison and weapons that destroy human and animal life. Finally, trading in slaves was prohibited.

"The Buddha mentioned many ways of losing wealth. They are debauchery, drunkenness, gambling, addiction to intoxicants, loitering unnecessarily in the streets at unsuitable hours, haunting fairs, gambling, and associating with evil companions and idle company. Furthermore, the Buddha advised us on the correct way of doing things, a way that fosters the development of both human beings and their societies. The Buddha taught people how to improve themselves materially as well as spiritually. He gave his advice equally to kings as well as to peasants."

At this point Reverend Muthima interrupted. "Isn't poverty a result of bad karma from an unwholesome past life, according to your religion?" he asked.

I replied that poverty might be a result either of a past karma, or of a present karma, or of both. But most karmas, according to the Buddha, can be supplanted by the wise and far-seeing decisions one makes in the present.

I continued. "The Buddha said, 'There are certain unwholesome karmas that can be suppressed and overcome by means of wise and strong steps taken in this life.[8] Furthermore he explained, 'Who once was heedless is heedless no more, brightens the world like the moon set free from clouds.'[9]

"Most often it is due to decisions made in the present life that past karma, good or bad, is able to rise up and find the opportunity to create its result. Therefore, the efforts that are made in present time are the preeminent causes of most people's gains or failures.

"Thus, it becomes clear to us that Buddhism is not a pessimistic religion. The Buddha explained how happiness is the natural result of having and using one's wealth wisely. He also explained how everyone could find happiness through the proper development of both themselves and society.

"Despite the misconception that Buddhism is only for those who renounce the world, Buddhism acknowledges that building up wealth is one of the fundamental activities of life. The Buddha himself even gave us many wise guidelines for properly acquiring wealth; however, he always stressed the point that the real reason for having wealth is to promote the development of higher human potential, and not for frivolous selfish pursuits."

Reverend Muthima replied, "My brother, I understand your philosophy and your practice a lot better now. The more I discuss Buddhism with you, even though I'm not sure if you'll make it to heaven, I am quite certain that you won't be going to hell."

I smiled at Reverend Muthima, who remains devoted to Christianity to this day.

> Speak the truth.
> Give whatever you can.
> Never be angry.
> These three practices will lead you
> Into the presence of the gods.[10]

THIRTEEN

Healing Powers
of Chanting

It is a tradition in Thailand, Burma, Cambodia, and Laos for males to enter the monastery and practice as novices for at least one week. This period may also last for as long as one year. It is believed that the men who undergo this training develop more well-rounded characters than those who do not.

One summer I was given four Thai novices to train for a week. Suwat, Vipa, Seevali, and Anando were in their mid-teens. Their parents confided in me that they were having some disciplinary problems with their sons. They were concerned that they would soon lose control of the boys, if they didn't learn personal responsibility and appropriate social and spiritual values. Because of their cultural background in Buddhist societies, the parents believed that it was only in the temple under the auspices of the *sangha* that their sons could develop these important traits.

When they arrived at the temple early in the morning, I gave the boys a pep talk on how to conduct themselves in the monastery, as well as on the importance and significance of the training they were about to undergo. There are also certain rituals that are involved in the ordination ceremony, which must be followed, and I explained these to the young men.

At ten o'clock in the morning the monks of the Vihara assembled in the Shrine Room and sat according to seniority. The parents of the four boys were already in the room, sitting on the floor. The candidates entered the room wearing the simple white robes of the novice and proceeded to offer flowers to the Buddha and to the monks. Then they joined their parents, knelt on the floor in the customary manner, and paid their respects to the Buddha and the members of the *sangha* by bowing three times to each. The senior monk then asked the boys if they had permission from their parents to become novices. At this point in the traditional ceremony, each young man formally asked permission from his parents to join the Order of Samanera, or novice monks. Afterward, each one bowed down before his parents three times. It was a proud and emotional moment for the parents as well as for the candidates.

The candidates left the Shrine Room accompanied by two monks who shaved their heads. Then they returned, carrying the eight articles necessary for a monk, which are the alms bowl, two robes, one under-robe, one belt, a sewing kit, a water strainer, and a razor.

The boys looked completely different with no hair, and I watched with amusement the parents' reactions to seeing their sons this way. The boys bowed before the *sangha*, and the most senior monk, assisted by another monk, began the ordination ceremony, which took approximately thirty minutes, including time for a blessing chant. Then the newly ordained novices took their places next to the *sangha* members. When they were seated on the dais, their parents came forward, presented gifts to their sons, and bowed before them three times.

The training period, which began immediately after the ceremony, went forward smoothly as planned. I started teaching them Pali chanting, the traditional form, which was originally chanted by the Buddha for the blessing and protection of his disciples and devotees. These *suttas,* or sermons in chanting form, were originally passed down orally. They were recorded on palm leaves about twenty-one hundred years ago and later compiled into books.

Paritta chanting is specifically for protecting ourselves from evil spirits, misfortune, sickness, and the negative influences of the planetary systems. *Paritta* chanting is practiced all over the world, especially in Theravada Buddhist countries. The first thing I taught the new novices were *Paritta* chants.[1] The rhythm of the chanting is important, and the vibrant sounds create a pleasant field of energy for the listeners as well as for the chanters.[2] The monks chant the *suttas* with various intonations to produce vibrations that can calm the mental state of all participants. When devoted and experienced monks chant with compassion and concentration, powerful thought and sound waves emit from their hearts, minds, and voices and touch the core beings of sincere listeners who are open to receiving their blessings.[3]

On one occasion when a child was reported to be under the influence of evil forces, the Buddha advised the monks to recite the *suttas* to ward off the evil forces.[4] When you learn and chant these *suttas,* their vibrations will be beneficial to you.

"May I ask you a question, Bhante?" asked Suwat very weakly.

"Yes, you may, Suwat," I replied.

"Bhante, you related what happened during the days of the Buddha. In your experience, have you or anyone else ever benefited from this chanting?"

"Of course, there have been many instances. As a matter

of fact, one particularly remarkable story about the results of chanting comes to mind."

Here is what I told Suwat:

It was the summer of 1976. I was seated on our lawn reading *What the Buddha Taught,* by Walpola Rahula, when an unshaven, ragged, young man approached me.

"I am Todd," he said, looking forlorn and almost gray. "I have a lot of problems—mental, physical, and personal. I lost my job, my wife is sick, and the Department of Social Services took away our children, as they believe we are not mentally stable enough to be parents. Is there any way you can help me?"

I felt sorry for him, and suddenly an idea came to me, which was to explain to him the benefits of chanting in our Buddhist tradition. I told him that there were two keys to make it work. First of all, he must have faith in my chanting, and secondly, I must exercise great compassion toward him. Otherwise, there would be no result. Todd said he was willing. I told him to visit me the next day between six and seven in the evening. I wasn't sure if he would show up, but when he did, I was happy to see him.

I took him to the Shrine Room, where I had already made preparations to chant *paritta.* I had a pot of water covered with a white cloth, and a string around the pot. This string was attached to the Buddha statue. Together, we held this string, and I chanted *paritta* for one hour. I noticed during the hour that Todd was uncomfortable and restless, probably wishing he hadn't come, but I could also see that he was determined to have faith in the results that I had told him would be produced. He was very desperate to find a cure for his plight.

I told Todd that we must continue this ritual for seven days. I knew that he needed time for the vibrations of the chanting to enter the center of his being and cause him to be healed. To my joy, when Todd came to the temple on the seventh day, he was a clean-shaven, well-dressed young man, who looked completely different from the depressed, ashen-colored person of a week before.

When our hour of chanting was over, I gave him the blessed water to drink and tied the blessed thread around his neck, rather than around his wrist, which is the usual custom. I felt that Todd still wasn't completely stable and needed the additional boost of energy and protection. He thanked me profusely, told me he felt much better, and said that he was determined to pull his life back together.

A few days later he returned to the temple and reported to me that he was physically and mentally strong again. He had stopped taking the medications his doctor had prescribed for him and there were tears of gratitude for my help.

Having himself been cured, he asked me if I could help his wife, believing that she was possessed by evil spirits. He couldn't talk her into coming to the temple, so he asked me to visit her with him at the couple's apartment. I was shocked to see her condition. Barbara lay on the floor, eyes closed, hands clasped as if in a trance. Her body was emaciated, and there were horrible odors in the room. Todd told me that she didn't open her eyes, because spirits troubled her. She was obviously delusional and paranoid.

I told her that the powers of the Buddha and his eternal truths would help her to recover. I further explained that the scientists who discovered atomic energy are no longer living, but that their knowledge of how to use it remains with us.

In the same manner, the Noble Teachings of the Buddha are most effective when chanted with feeling and compassion, bringing blessings to the believer.[5] I said to her, "I will chant *paritta* to remove all evil forces that are hindering you and making you fearful. Please believe in what I am doing and listen closely to my chanting with a positive attitude. You will soon feel better."

I chanted. Gradually, she seemed to relax. I visited her two more times and chanted *paritta* in her presence. On the third day I carried a statue of the Buddha with me, which I placed on a stool near her bed. I completed my chanting, lifted up the statue, and called to her.

I said, "Barbara, the *suttas* that I chanted were originally delivered by the Buddha. He was the embodiment of compassion, love, and all the virtues that he preached. Please open your eyes and look at the compassionate face of the Buddha."

She slowly opened her eyes and gazed at the Perfected One. She screamed with joy, "I am free. I am released," and stood up near her husband. They embraced one another shedding tears of happiness.

A few months later Todd and Barbara visited me. They were very happy to tell me that they had regained custody of their children. I was glad to hear that Todd had obtained a professorial position in a well-known university.

We have maintained our friendship over the years. Todd is now following the Buddha's teachings, and remains faithful to me and our temple, never forgetting to support us whenever there is a need. Today, Todd has one of the highest positions in the world in his field and has written more than one hundred books.

Seevali, Suwat, Anando, and Vipa were amazed to hear this powerful story. I believe it made an impression on the young novices, because they seemed to be full of questions. Vipa started by saying, "How can you cure a physical ailment by chanting *paritta*?"

I replied, "According to the teachings of the Buddha, the mind is closely linked with the body. He taught that the mental state of an individual dramatically affects the physical well-being of that person. Modern psychologists support the Buddha's view, having proved that the body slows down when the mind slows down. Psychologists and

Buddhists agree that an optimistic person has better chances of recovery due to his or her positive attitude, and contrarily, a pessimistic person lessens the chances of recovery due to his or her negative attitude. Chanting contributes the additional benefits of providing emotional comfort to the individual and, at the same time, helps reduce stress. It goes without saying that one must develop the proper attitude of faith and virtue in order to obtain the best results from chanting. And of course, common sense must lead one to seek proper medical attention if one is injured or seriously ill."

Seevali seemed to be restless, so I asked him what was bothering him.

"Bhante, I can't sit still even for five minutes. How can I concentrate to listen to you?"

"Seevali, you obviously need to develop your powers of concentration. To do that you must believe in what you are doing, knowing that it is correct. The chanting of *suttas* can bring material blessings if the listeners maintain the appropriate wholesome state of mind combined with confidence in the outcome. According to the Buddha, right effort is a necessary factor in overcoming suffering. Seevali, while you are here at the Vihara this week, I challenge you to make the effort to learn to sit still. Only then can you begin to increase your ability to concentrate."

I continued by telling the young men that all *suttas* have intrinsic powers because the Buddha's teachings, as well as his *paritta* chantings, are assertions or affirmations of truth. At the end of the recital of each *sutta*, the chanters bless the listeners with the words, *"Etena saccha vacchena sothi te hotu sabbada,"* which means, "By the power of the truth of these words, may you ever be well."

When our talk was over and I was getting ready to leave, Anando stopped me.

"Bhante, I doubt whether I could memorize all those

words. Could you teach me a short verse to overcome my dreadful dreams?" Anando had more than once during the week he was at the Vihara awakened in the middle of the night choking and screaming. Each time, one of the monks would rush to his side and comfort him.

"Anando, I am glad you asked me that question. When I was a novice, I had bad dreams, too. My teacher taught me to recite verse 183 from the Dhammapada seven times. It really worked for me. Why don't you try to learn it and see if it helps you:

> *Sabba-papassa akaranam,*
> *Kusalassa upasampada,*
> *Sacitta-pariyodapanam.*
> *Etam buddhana-sasanam.*[6]

Which means:

> The non-doing of all evil,
> The performance of what is good,
> The cleansing of one's own mind:
> This is the Buddha's teaching.

Anando was disturbed by his nighttime episodes and promised me that he would never sleep without reciting this *sutta*. I saw him earlier this year and he told me that he has never missed a night, and his bad dreams have never returned.

The week's training period went fast. I noticed that the novices' stay at the Vihara, and the training in mindfulness that they had undergone, seemed to have matured them to some extent. It was evident to me that they had made progress in the development of a positive mental attitude as well as a desire to cultivate wholesome, productive thoughts. Occasionally they still visit me at the Vihara accompanied by their parents. Their parents believe that the training was truly beneficial to their sons and have noticed a remarkable change in attitude, which they feel makes them more trustworthy and responsible, no longer in danger of going out of control.

FOURTEEN

The London Doctor

It was late in the night. I was in my room when the telephone rang. When I answered, I heard a woman sobbing hysterically and talking in Bengali. I could not understand clearly what she was saying. I asked her to stop crying and to tell me her troubles. She calmed down and spoke to me in English. At that moment I knew it was Gita, Dr. Barua's daughter, whom I'd known in Calcutta.

Gita and her husband Ravi's parents had the same surname, Barua, which in Bengali means "Buddhist." They were all close associates of mine years before when I was living in Calcutta. Dr. Ravi Barua and Gita had since taken up residence in Los Angeles and were frequent visitors to my temple.

Gita had often complained that her husband believed everything his mother said as though it were written in stone. That night on the phone she said that her life was miserable and that she couldn't live with Ravi anymore. I did my best to calm her down, told her to be a little patient, and to visit me the following morning with her husband.

The next morning Gita arrived with Ravi and related her side of the story in his presence.

Before she began, Gita shifted her weight in the chair. She seemed nervous, but anxious to speak. "Bhante," she said. "May I speak freely?"

I asked Ravi how he felt. He nodded, Yes. I indicated to Gita that she could continue.

"Well, Bhante, in the early 1970s Ravi graduated from medical college in Calcutta and married me. We were very excited about making a life together. He was accepted for a residency in England, so shortly after the wedding we moved to London to make a new life. There were some difficulties in the beginning of our life together, but many newlyweds have these same problems. My husband tried, but couldn't acquire a scholarship, and the Indian government at that time didn't allow anyone to take money out of the country."

"How did you manage?" I asked.

"We arrived in London with a limited amount of funds. We had budgeted our meager resources well enough to acquire a tiny apartment near the hospital."

"That sounds convenient," I said. "Please continue."

"I managed to find a clerical job to make ends meet. My mother-in-law was naturally worried, and she constantly phoned to see how things were going. Why did she have to phone all the time? She knew that her son was not eating properly, because he did not know how to cook like the typical Indian man. She also knew that I was working outside the home full-time as the breadwinner. These ideas kept building up in her mind until she could no longer stand the pressure of her own thoughts."

"Every mother feels that way, Gita. What is wrong with that?" I asked.

"Well, one day she flew to London. She moved into our tiny apartment immediately. She believed that her presence would be of great benefit to her son, and she justified it by saying that I obviously needed her help."

"How did you take her being there?"

"I took it in good faith. I never complained that there was not enough room, or that I felt cramped at all by my husband's mom. But the tension was most certainly there, in that tiny apartment. Each morning his mom would fix a cup of tea for him, but not for me. Yet I said nothing. Mom would fix breakfast, because, of course, I had to leave for work. When I managed to squeeze in cooking a meal after my long day, she always complained. It was too salty, too fatty, my mother had not taught me how to cook, and I should learn from her how to cook the way her son liked it. She went on and on. She kept nagging, but I never complained."

"Gita, you sound like you tried to be patient with her in a difficult situation. What happened next?" I asked.

"His mother often warned me not to get pregnant. She said her son was almost finished with his first year of residency, and that she was glad I was helping. But she said it would ruin everything if I got pregnant and couldn't work. 'You'd both have to go back to India!' she said. Yet I remained silent, never showing disrespect. But his mother was definitely in my space! His mother became so worried about the potential disaster of a pregnancy that she moved from the couch and began to sleep in our bed, between us."

Ravi began to look very uncomfortable. Pretty soon he stood up and began to walk out of the room.

"Ravi," I called to him. "I am your family counselor. Please come back and let's work this out. You don't have to be embarrassed." I held his hand as he sat down again next to Gita.

Ravi spoke. "Bhante," he explained, "this was for our own good; a pregnancy would have hurt us badly."

Gita spoke up. "Bhante, I complained to Ravi that the situation with his mother was getting out of hand. I told him that although I respected and loved his mother and knew that she meant well, married couples simply should not have their in-laws sleeping with them. But it was to no avail. Mom was there to stay."

"Gita, please tell me more about how you feel," I said calmly.

"Okay, Bhante," she replied, and then, after a pause, she continued. "I was hoping that the situation would solve itself in due course. I thought in time my husband would graduate and we would get a bigger apartment. And eventually, his mother would have to go back to India. But the situation got worse as time went on. Somehow my cooking, even with my best efforts, did not improve in her opinion. My husband started to agree, even though everyone else seemed to love my cooking. And I received no recognition for anything I did. Ravi's mother didn't 'believe' in celebrating events such as birthdays or anniversaries. She thought that with our limited income, a card or flowers was a waste of money and precious time. And she convinced her son of that, too. I didn't want to make trouble, but I felt hurt on each birthday or anniversary. Ravi never said a word about my birthday! I would say, 'Do you know what day it is?' always to be greeted with the reply that I shouldn't be so silly, that every day was special.

"Ravi eventually passed his examinations and became an M.D. Seeking greater opportunities, he and I moved to the United States. To my delight, within a year I conceived and gave birth to a baby girl, and the following year a baby boy. No sooner had we gotten settled than his mother joined us. Now our troubles are multiplying because of her interference in our lives." Gita burst out crying.

"Ravi, what have you to say?" I asked.

Ravi replied, "Bhante, Gita fails to think about the fact

that my mother is a widow. She struggled to bring up her children and was determined to see that I became a medical doctor. I recall the sleepless nights she had when I was studying for my exams. She was the last to sleep and the first to get up to prepare our breakfast, which was usually very frugal. She washed and ironed our clothes. She made our lives comfortable by making many sacrifices.

"One day I noticed that my mother was not eating, though she had served us our food. When I walked into the kitchen, I noticed that there was no food for her to eat except the roasted rice at the bottom of the pan." Tears rolled down Ravi's cheeks, and there was a moment of silence.

Finally he continued as I listened patiently. "Bhante, you know that there is no one more important than one's mother. I have only one mother and no one can replace her; but a wife can always be replaced."

Gita just stared at him, not believing that her husband could say something so cruel.

An uncomfortable moment passed, and Ravi spoke again. "In Sunday school we learn that Brahma, our Hindu Creator God, is equal to our parents. We also learn that Brahma has four sublime states: the first is loving kindness, the second is compassion, the third is appreciative joy, and the fourth is equanimity. All of these qualities are embodied in every parent.[1] Don't you agree?"

"Well," I replied, taking a pause, knowing I had to advise and console both parties. "Ravi, let us discuss the sublime states that you just mentioned." Ravi and Gita both looked at me with interest. "The love of the sublime states can be experienced in our daily life. Parents project loving kindness toward their children. They wish for their children to enjoy good health, have good friends, be intelligent, and be successful in all of their endeavors. In the same manner, a practicing Buddhist should show his or her love to all living beings. Ravi, I am sorry to say, your mother is a wonderful lady, yet her loving kindness is mixed up with personal affections."

"What do you mean by that?" questioned Ravi.

"Your mother thinks that she has to love only you. Not also your wife. Pure universal love, which we call *metta,* is different. It is firm, but not grasping. It is unshakable, but not tied down. It is gentle and not hard. It is helpful, but not interfering. It is dignified, but not proud. It is active, not passive. Universal love is released without any restrictions. It gives calm, peace, and unity. It also gives us right understanding, right thought, right speech, right action, right livelihood, right effort, right mindfulness, and right concentration. Furthermore, universal love teaches us to be hospitable and charitable to one another. It teaches us to speak pleasantly and agreeably to one another. It teaches us not to quarrel among ourselves, but to work for each other's welfare."

Ravi and Gita remained silent, but occasionally glanced toward one another.

"In the same manner, compassion, or *karuna,* must be cultivated. When parents see their children seriously ill, they will naturally be moved by compassion and an earnest wish that the child be free from the suffering brought on by illness. In the same way, we have to experience feelings of compassion when witnessing the suffering of all living beings.

"I remember a Japanese Buddhist story from which I have learned a lesson. There was a well-known teacher who had a three-month retreat attended by exactly five hundred students. Among them was a kleptomaniac. The students who participated in the retreat kept losing their belongings and finally complained to the teacher about the suspected culprit. The teacher, however, took no action. Eventually the students decided to sign a petition and submitted it to the teacher. It stated that if the teacher didn't take any action, they would all leave the retreat. The teacher noticed that there were 499 signatures. He called upon everyone and said, 'I received the petition signed by all of you except one. All 499 of you are virtuous people with principles. You can exist anywhere in the world without causing any trouble to others, or getting into trouble yourselves. I am confident that you will all be assets to society; therefore, if you leave, you have my blessings. I do not have to worry about you. However, the one person who has not signed this petition needs my help. He must stay with me. If he leaves, he will be a hindrance to society and eventually end up a criminal.'[2]

"Like this teacher, whose compassion was distributed equally toward the uplifting of all human beings, we must also learn to extend our compassion to the needy, and not only to the one or ones we love most."

Gita spoke up and said, "I just wish your mother could exercise a little compassion toward me."

Ravi said nothing.

I continued. "Ravi, the third sympathetic state is *mudita*, which means sympathetic joy or appreciative joy. It is the wholesome attitude of rejoicing in the happiness of all human beings. It makes people less self-centered, and it eliminates jealousy. Appreciative joy is like a mother's joy at her son's success and happiness."

"That's all my mother was trying to express, Gita. She wanted to show her joy!" Gita just looked at her husband in dismay, seeing that he was missing the point.

"The fourth sublime state is the wholesome attitude of *upekkha*, or equanimity, which counters clinging and aversion. When a son gets married and begins to lead an independent life, his mother still has the feeling of loving kindness, compassion, and appreciative joy for him, but with no interfering or attachment. These qualities are combined with a feeling of equanimity, or equal feeling for all. Equanimity is the condition that promotes impartiality toward everyone, complete detachment. When it is practiced, both aversion and attachment are eradicated."[3]

Gita interrupts, "That's exactly what I mean. His mother appreciates only what he does, not what I do, or what our children do."

I replied, "Gita, you should understand that your mother-in-law is not an enlightened being. She is just an ordinary person who has made a lot of sacrifices in her life to bring up her children. Unfortunately, she does not understand the difference between *metta*, loving kindness, and *pema*, personal affection. Her personal affection has shrouded her loving kindness; therefore she appreciates only her son. That is human nature. Humans are irrational animals, and the animal nature will arise in an undeveloped mind. Even a cow will protect its calf from harm. In order to protect the newborn, she will be defensive even when her master comes to feed her. Gita, think about yourself. You love your children more than your relatives."

"I understand you, Bhante," said Gita. "Ravi takes me to all his friends' birthday celebrations; we take gifts as well. But for my birthday, he doesn't even give me good wishes, much less a gift."

"I have heard this complaint on innumerable occasions," I replied. "Unfortunately, some Buddhists are concerned only about the monks' code of discipline; they are unaware that the Buddha expounded a code of rules for both men and women. Ravi, I am surprised that you completely ignore Gita's birthdays. The Buddha himself has advised a husband to remember such occasions."

"Bhante, in which book has he said so?" asked Ravi.

"It is in the *Digha Nikaya Sigalovada Sutta,* and I'll tell you the story. One day, the Buddha saw a young man named Sigala bowing to the six directions. When the Buddha questioned Sigala about his practice, Sigala replied that his father requested him to do so on his deathbed.[4]

"Sigala said, 'Why, Lord Buddha, does my father want me to do this practice?' The Buddha answered by saying that there are six types of human relationships, characterized by the six directions.

"First of all, he said that the east represents the parents. He chose the east for the parents because the sun comes up early and rises in the east, bringing light and life to all.

"The west represents the spouse because the sun sets in the west, and until life ends, husband and wife live together in harmony.

"The north represents friends and friendship, because magnetic north is the attractive force that draws friends together.

"The south represents the teachers because the sun's light is the brightest when it comes from the south; therefore, the wisdom is the strongest.

"Then there is the above, or the sky, which represents religious teachings, which can be characterized as being endless and as being the bearers of peace and wisdom, and the foundation for the path to enlightenment.

"Finally there is the below, or the earth, which represents the foundation of all worldly things. Here the Buddha speaks about honoring employees and the other support people who hold it all up; without earth, no one would be able to stand.

"Therefore, honoring the six directions means fulfilling one's reciprocal responsibilities.

"Marriage is a partnership. Living in the same house with someone for many years is not easy; it requires skill, patience, and compassion. A husband and wife form the nucleus of the family. Their harmonious and successful marriage brings stability to the family. It will also have a happy effect on the children."[5]

After a brief pause I continued, "The Buddha taught us that an ideal marriage can be achieved if a husband shows love and respect for his wife by being courteous to her, appreciating her, being faithful to her, sharing authority with her in family matters, and giving her presents on special occasions. In return, the wife should reciprocate with love and respect for her husband and support him by managing the household well, being hospitable to his friends and relatives, being faithful to him, taking care of the wealth of the family, and being industrious in her work."[6]

Gita and Ravi both had tears in their eyes. "Bhante," they both said at the same time, and smiled.

Ravi nudged Gita softly to speak first. "I never heard of such a beautiful way a couple should be together."

Ravi immediately added, "Amazing, simply amazing. I am beginning to see for the first time how I might build a happy life with Gita!"

Gita spoke up and said, "But what is going to happen about the situation with your mother? I truly can't go on this way."

Ravi had a look on his face that told me he didn't have an answer. I said, "I truly think that your mother is unhappy here in America. She is far away from her other children in Calcutta, and she is, perhaps, too old to adapt to a new culture. Now that you are settled down here in California with a successful practice, perhaps you could suggest to your mother that she might be happier with your sister Depa in India. You could visit her every year, and send Depa money to help support her."

Ravi looked sad about the possibility of being so far away from his mother, but he also realized that what I had suggested was the only hope for his marriage. "I will do as you say, Bhante." In fact, it worked out just this way.

> One by one, little by little, moment
>   by moment,

A wise person should remove his or her
    impurities
As a silversmith removes the impurities
    from silver.[7]

Focus, not on the rudeness of others,
not on what they've done
    or left undone,
but on what you
have and haven't done
    yourself.[8]

FIFTEEN

Children Change Us

For many years I have worked with the Cambodian community as a religious adviser and mentor. Cambodian people have an extended family system that is very supportive of each individual within the family unit. Unfortunately, when they migrate to the United States, which has a nuclear family system, they find it very difficult to adjust to the way families interact here.

Kalya and her family often visit my temple. Several years ago there was a period during which she complained about her eldest daughter, Vanni, every time she saw me. Vanni was an eighteen-year-old who had overstepped the boundaries established by her family, eager to adopt the freedom enjoyed by her American peers. She had become a night owl, was irresponsible about keeping her commitments, refused to do her share of the household chores, and didn't want her parents to meet her boyfriend. In fact, she had become a problem to her family.

Kalya was worried because Vanni was setting a bad example for her younger sisters. Kalya had been a teacher in

Cambodia, where teachers have the authority to correct and punish the children, and she was a strict disciplinarian. She wanted her children to be brought up in the tradition of sharing the responsibilities of a united family.

And like any other mother, Kalya also wanted her children to be educated and to enjoy the benefits of their new country. Kalya's husband, Vipa, was very passive; he ceded all authority to his wife and agreed to abide by her decisions.

One day I received a call from Kalya saying that Vanni had moved out of the house and was living with her girlfriend in a rented apartment. The family could not accept their daughter moving out of the family home until she was married. They were devastated and felt disgraced in the eyes of their Cambodian culture. Kalya wanted me to advise Vanni and persuade her to move back home.

I set up an appointment for the family to visit me, and I personally called Vanni to make sure she would also be there. When we met in the Shrine Room of my temple, I could feel the hostile energy between the family and their estranged daughter. Kalya and Vanni wouldn't even look one another in the eye. Each was convinced she was right, and they made no attempt to conceal their anger.

I turned to Vanni and asked her to tell her side of the story first. I listened with an open mind.

"My mother abuses me!" was the first statement that came out of her mouth.

"What do you mean by abuse, Vanni?" I asked her, never believing that Kalya would physically harm any of her children.

"She has a list of chores for me to do every day. She wants me to clean the bathrooms, clean the kitchen floor, launder my sisters' clothes, and vacuum the entire house once a week," she replied, looking as victimized as she could.

"Is that all?" I exclaimed. "Vanni, that's not abuse."

The young girl ignored my comment and continued.

"When I return home late, she shouts at me. She always wants to know where I went, who I went with, and what I did. She pokes her nose into my personal business, and she's a pain."

"Vanni," I began patiently. "I can cite a story from Buddhist literature that might help us understand this situation better. One day, Prince Abhayaraja questioned the Buddha about some remarks he had made that had hurt the feelings of his brother-in-law Devadatta. Devadatta was at this time also a disciple of the Buddha.

"The Buddha replied, 'Prince, I speak the truth as it is, but I never say harsh things to anyone. If the infant you are holding in your arms were to put a pebble in his mouth, what would you do?'

"The Prince answered, 'I would take out the pebble, of course.'

"The Buddha responded, 'What if it were not so easy to take it out?'

"'Then I would hold the child still and put my finger in his mouth and find the pebble and pull it out,' replied the Prince.

"Then the Buddha asked, 'When you do that, won't it hurt the child?'

"'Yes, Sir, it will hurt the child, but it is necessary to save his life.'

"'In the same way, when I speak the truth as it really is, some people may feel hurt, and some may even get angry. However, I do not say these things to hurt them, but because of the limitless compassion I feel for them.'[1]

"Do you understand what the Buddha meant by this statement, Vanni?"

Vanni just looked at me and shrugged her shoulders, not seeming to care about what I had said. I said, "Your parents cannot sleep when you are out late at night. When they watch the TV news I am sure they get worried about you. Often the news is of murder, rape, rave parties, drug binges, drunk driving, and so forth—any or all of which, in their imagination, could happen to you.

"Vanni, you come from a good Buddhist family. You should be aware that the Buddha strongly advised his followers to avoid unnecessary outings in the night. In the *Sigalovada Sutta* he said,

> Young householder, there are these six evil consequences of a person sauntering in streets at unseemly hours: he himself becomes unprotected and unguarded; his wife and children become unprotected and unguarded; his property becomes unprotected and unguarded; he becomes suspected of committing crimes and evil deeds; he becomes subjected to false accusations; he will have to face many troubles. Young householder, these are the six evil consequences of sauntering in streets at unseemly hours.²"

I looked at Vanni and I could tell that she still wasn't getting my message. I continued by saying, "Do you know what difficulties a mother goes through to bring up a child? It is from conception that she takes care of her unborn. All her energies are directed toward the child, even before its birth. To see to the comforts of the child, the parents spend restless nights, at times for months on end. They undergo immense pain, which is borne silently, to nurse and bring up their children.

"Children are indeed a source of delight and happiness to their parents, but raising them is by no means an easy task. I had an experience that helped me realize how difficult a parent's job is. I'd like to share this true story with you.

"Over two decades ago, a young Sri Lankan couple came to visit me in my humble first temple, which was located in Hollywood. At that time, there was only me and my friend Bhante Ananda. This couple were students at the time, they didn't know many people, and they had little money. They had no one else to call upon, so they asked us to take care of their six-month-old baby for a couple of hours while they attended to some urgent business. I was delighted to be the baby-sitter, as I had never had the opportunity to do this before. My friend Bhante Ananda wasn't too happy about taking on this responsibility, but he reluctantly gave in.

"Just a few minutes after the couple left, the baby started to cry. I tried my best to quiet him by carrying him while pacing up and down the hallway. I talked, I sang, I even chanted. I did everything I could think of to make him stop crying, but nothing worked.

"My friend thought the baby might be hungry and suggested we try giving him some milk. Then we wondered whether to heat the milk or give it to him cold. Finally, we decided to boil the milk.

"By this time we were getting frantic, since the baby was screaming at the top of his lungs. In my excitement, I dropped the bottle and it broke. My friend started to laugh. Somehow we had to feed the baby. All of a sudden an idea dawned on me. I remembered how as little children we used to feed baby squirrels in Sri Lanka. We made cotton wicks, dipped them in the milk, and let the squirrels suck them.

"So we applied the same technique and calmed the child. This incident enlightened me as to how difficult it is to bring up a child.

"Your mother had to take care of four children, Vanni. I sympathize with her, knowing what a hard time she had. I want you to read these two letters sent by an American devotee to her parents. She specifically mentioned that I have her permission to use these letters whenever an appropriate occasion arises." I handed her the two letters, which I will reproduce here.

Dearest Dad,

You have been the light of strength for me. In your struggle to provide a home for all of us, you suffered separation. You worked long hours, traveled far from your home, and then returned, sometimes without recognition from your children. You never expected it or did it for recognition. You did it because of your love. You did not receive the credit and warmth deserved at times from me. You withdrew and had a hard time showing how much you loved us all and loved me. I know you loved me. I know you love me now, with all your heart. Your love and life brought me to LIFE. It enfolded me, and through your example, I was able to connect—as I have—to the beauty of the Sacred. What an amazing gift. You are beautiful beyond words. All along the way, you have supported me and loved me even when it was not easy to do so. Sometimes, everyone else shared his or her love with Mom, and you were left without a hug, whether physical or emotional. I know that must have been difficult, because you have done everything in your life to help and support us. You were the one that supported me, not only through trusts of money, but in the unconditional trust of love. That was you who did that.

Eventually, you withdrew because you didn't want me or others to know how alone you felt. I still loved you even in hard times, but didn't always show it to you. I want to say to you now that I know who you are and recognize the beauty and strength and wisdom that you are. I have wept to think that you would not know this. I have cried out in prayer that you could feel and experience the joy of my life because of what you did for me to be here, whether conscious or unconscious, that's what you did, and what your father did, and his father.

I am in full amazement of the strength and beauty of your love and commitment to my happiness and me. I am weeping with joy right now at the thought. I thank you with all my heart and soul, for all the love you are, completely and without condition.

Thank you, dearest Dad, for your love, strength, light, lessons, patience, support, laughter, throwing me up in the air as a girl to allow me to reach for the sky and to find my way home. For all the times you lent a guiding hand, the times you picked me up when I fell, the pony rides on your lap, the debates between us to sharpen my mind, the loving support of who you truly are. I want you to know, I am home, surrounded by love, warmed by the fires of life, secure in the knowing of the Sacred Presence, and now I will never be alone again. This is because of your love. I will never leave you, for you are in my heart forever. I know you never left me, you were always there as a loving guide. Thank you, dearest Dad. Thank you with all my heart!

With Deepest Eternal Love,

Your Daughter

Dearest Mom,

I have never known one such as you. You think that your mother was greater than you. This is not Truth. You are as great a mom to me as your mother was to you. For, whenever I was lost, whenever I cried out to find my way, there you were to remind me of who I was, and to show me with your deep and everlasting love the beauty of life, just with the example of being yourself. You enfolded me in your loving arms and heart and kept me nourished with the light of your love. I know it has not been easy. I am constantly amazed that you had four children in four years! How did you do it? Now I know it was because of your strength and love. And you did it with grace and balance, and a constant supply of loving kindness.

I am looking in words to describe a way to thank you, and the deepest word is my unconditional love and admiration for who you are. I recognize you. I see your beauty. I know, and want to bathe you in a nectar of love, dearest Mother, for the gift of who you have been and are to me. I know I have not been an easy job, yet you never felt that way, even when you stayed up nights and were tired. Even when you did without so we could have. Your love shone through and was my anchoring. All the joy, love, laughter, and light of my life are because of you. I would literally have died from sadness on several occasions if your loving voice had not pulled me though. I now know the greatest joy, and my heart is full of Love and the Sacredness of the Source of All. This is because of you and your mom and her mom. You showed me who I am with your love. Your hard work, devotion, and sacrifice allowed for the river of love to flow into my heart, and I am restored. How could I ever thank you enough?

One day, or maybe now, you will know completely that what I say is Truth. This brings me, again, greatest happiness. Are you my Santa Claus? Thank you, sweetest and dearest one, with all my heart.

With all Love, deepest Love, sweetest Love,

Your Daughter

I observed Vanni while she was reading the letters. I noticed a distinct change in her countenance, but she remained silent and still wouldn't look directly at her mother or father.

I then took the opportunity to express my opinion about how to adjust to living in American society. I spoke to Kalya and advised her to learn how to express her affection for her children, both verbally and physically. I am aware that it is not something that is practiced in their Cambodian culture, but since we are bringing up children in America, we should exhibit our affection toward them the way the Americans do. This, I said, applied to the father as well. In the Asian culture, the children bow before their parents and venerate them before they leave the house and before they go to sleep. In the Western world children show their affection by hugging and kissing their parents. If the old Asian customs no longer work in this country, then we must develop a happy medium that somehow absorbs American values.

At this point Vanni got up to go and said that she would call me. The family left the temple with my blessings.

A few weeks later I was relieved to see the family at the temple. They all seemed quite cheerful, so I knew Vanni's problem was probably solved.

The Buddha's words rang in my ears:

Even if the children carry
    on the right shoulder,
        Mother and
    on the left shoulder,
        Father
Fulfilling all their parents' needs
    for a hundred years.
They still cannot compensate
    for the debt they owe their parents.[3]

SIXTEEN

The Alcoholic

Early one Saturday morning, even before the birds began to sing, my telephone rang, startling me. I knew it had to be some sort of an emergency, so I picked it up immediately.

The call was from Calcutta, and it turned out to be Devi, wife of the late Dr. Chaudari. Dr. Chaudari had been a pillar of strength during my stay in Calcutta. It was he who introduced me to Mother Teresa, to whom I gave my voluntary services.

Devi sounded depressed, and she complained about her son, Anup. The young man, unfortunately, had not been able to recover from the shock of his father's death, and he had picked up the habit of drowning his sorrows in alcohol. Devi said she was unable to control him, and she begged me for my help. She believed that if she sent Anup to America his problem would be solved. I promised to think about her son's condition and said I would call her in a few days.

I decided that I must help Anup. I knew that he had received his education in Houston, Texas. He was married and had a child, so it appeared that things were settled for him. Secretly, however, he was a very troubled man who drank heavily. His wife, Lakshmi, was quickly losing her patience because of his continual use of alcohol.

Eventually, the couple decided that a new start was the only way to solve Anup's problem. They sold everything they owned and returned to India to be nearer to their families.

Anup got a good job in India, but unfortunately things did not work out as they had planned. Anup returned to his drinking habits and eventually had to sell his house to pay debts. His wife finally divorced him and retained custody of his only son, Ravi. The two of them moved to the United States. Anup had lost his job, his wife, and his son. This plunged him into an even deeper depression.

The day after I received Devi's phone call from Calcutta I called Lakshmi, who was living in San Diego. Her replies to my questions about a possible reconciliation were negative. I had the feeling that she had totally given up on him, as she said that only a miracle could change him.

I took it upon myself to help Anup. I called his mother and strongly suggested that she enroll her son in an Alcoholics Anonymous program. A few months later she called me and said that Anup was sober. She asked me whether I could help him get a new start in the United States.

Shortly afterward, to my surprise, Anup's sister, Deepali, who lives in Sydney, Australia, gave me a call. She told me glowing things about her brother, who, she said, had gotten over his drinking habit. A few weeks later I received a letter from Anup stating that he would be arriving in Los Angeles and asking me to pick him up at the airport.

On the day of Anup's arrival I drove to Los Angeles International Airport and waited for him at the gate. I stood there until the last person got off the plane, but I didn't see him. I spoke to the airline agent at the desk and he confirmed that Anup had indeed been on the flight and had arrived safely in Los Angeles. I returned to the Vihara, but felt very concerned about what might have happened to him. Two days later Anup showed up at the temple while I was away and demanded that the monks pay the taxi fare, which was $250. The monks paid the taxi driver because they knew Anup was the abbot's friend.

When I arrived I was relieved to see Anup. Later, after talking to him, I realized that he was drunk. "Forgive me, Bhante, but I drink because my wife, Lakshmi, won't let me see my only son." He put his head in his hands and began to weep, causing me to feel great pity for him.

I decided that under the circumstances, the best thing would be for him to stay at the temple. The next day, when he had sobered up, I told him that if he wanted my help, he had no choice but to enter an Alcoholics Anonymous program. He reluctantly agreed.

About an hour later I checked him into a rehabilitation center in the Crenshaw area for a thirty-day detox program. I told Anup to cooperate with the medical personnel and to do his best to overcome his addiction. I also told him that I would be back every two or three days to see how he was. Much to my surprise, later that evening he somehow found his way back to the temple.

"What are you doing back here so soon, Anup? I told you to stay there for thirty days!" I exclaimed.

"I can't help it, Bhante. I started feeling sick, and I wanted to see my son." He broke down in tears and started crying uncontrollably.

"I told you, Anup, that the only way Lakshmi will allow you to see your son again is if you are completely free of alcohol. Does the bottle mean more to you than your only son? Don't you have any feeling for your family?"

"I am just a weak man, Bhante. I don't think I can be free of this problem."

I really didn't know what to do with Anup. I suddenly thought about one of our members, named Dede, who lived not far from the temple in the Wilshire district. Dede is a female Theravada Buddhist who also practices Reiki and other healing arts combined with hypnosis and meditation techniques. I called her on the phone and asked her to please come right over.

The three of us gathered in the Shrine Room, and Dede listened intently to Anup's sad story. She also was moved by his pathetic condition and then hypnotized him and gave him posthypnotic suggestions that would support him in abstaining from alcohol. After he came out of the hypnotic state, Dede counseled him and gave him positive affirmations that he could use when he felt himself succumbing to his desires.

In the evening Anup joined us in meditation. After a few minutes he jumped up from his cushion and let out a shriek, saying that there was a snake crawling around the meditation hall. He ran over to the monk who was presiding over the meditation and said, "Can't you see the cobra? He's going to bite you!" When the monk remained silent in meditation, Anup shouted, "Okay, you stupid monk, I don't care if you die!" and then he ran out of the room.

Anup's outburst and sudden departure left the rest of us a bit shaken, but we knew that he was hallucinating. Dede and I kept calm and didn't try to stop him.

Later, I called him to come down to the dining room where there was food left over from lunchtime. When he sat down to the table I noticed that his hands were shaking so badly that he was unable to hold a fork, and he complained that he had no appetite. By this time he hadn't shaved or changed clothes in about four days, so he looked absolutely terrible. I gave him some vitamins to take, telling him that he would get even sicker without some sort of nourishment, but he refused to take them.

"Has my aunt been here to see me? My mother used to try to poison me with pills like those. I'm sure my mother sent poison to my aunt to give to me. She wants me to die!"

I was simply flabbergasted and told him that he shouldn't say such outrageous things against his own mother and her sister. "You can take the pills or not, Anup," I told him, "Because if you die, you will only have yourself to blame."

"Okay, Bhante, because you are a monk I trust you," and then he swallowed the tablets. Afterward he got up from the table and went back upstairs without another word.

At midnight I heard a thundering knock on my door. I asked who it was, and Anup answered. I opened the door and he screamed at me, "I know you are poisoning me, just like my mother. Why does everyone want to poison me?" he kept asking over and over again.

Exasperated, I told him to get back to his room. He turned around and walked back down the hall muttering to himself, but by this time I was too upset to sleep. About an hour later I checked his room and saw that he wasn't there. I looked all over the temple for him, but he was nowhere to be found.

In the early hours of the morning I heard a huge ruckus coming from outside on the sidewalk in front of the temple. I looked out the window and saw that it was Anup demonstrating, walking back and forth outside the fence, right on Crenshaw Boulevard. He was shouting at the top of his voice, asking passersby in their cars to help the Alcoholics Anonymous program. "Please give money to AA, they need your money!" He was also saying things about the powers of the monks. "Last night this huge tree was only a seedling. Look at it now! These monks have blessed it and made it grow in only one night!"

No one could get him to stop demonstrating and carrying on in such an unseemly manner in front of our temple. Finally, someone called the police. I realized that nothing could help Anup but a detoxification program in the hospital. While I was driving him to the hospital at USC, Anup kept telling me that he wanted me to take him to the police station.

He said, "I want to file a formal complaint against those people. I am especially going to press charges against that white devil lady, Dede. Every time I tried to go into a bar last night she was standing in the doorway laughing at me and taunting me. She kept me from going inside and getting a drink!" He was obviously referring to a posthypnotic suggestion planted by Dede the evening before. Apparently it had worked!

I used a bit of psychology myself and asked him, "Why aren't you filing an action against your mother? She's the one you said had poisoned you."

He lashed out at me like a tiger, screaming, "What kind of monk are you? How dare you tell a son to go up against his own mother and press police charges!"

I was amazed that even in his state of alcoholic dementia he could still defend his mother with such great respect. Once we got to the hospital, he adamantly told the admitting nurse that I had poisoned him. The hospital authorities questioned me, but never seriously thought I was guilty of any crime, given Anup's obvious deranged mental condition.

A few weeks passed, and one day Anup returned to the temple to see me. I was very pleased to see that he was a sober man.

"I am sorry, Bhante, for all the trouble I caused you. Please forgive me." Once again he put his head in his hands and wept, but this time it was for a different reason.

"Anup, of course I forgive you, and you can stay here at the temple until you find employment. However, I am not the person you should be asking to forgive you. You need to seek the forgiveness of Lakshmi, Ravi, and your mother. You need to make an attempt to put things right with them, if it's not too late. Now that you seem to be on the road to recovery, I will tell you what the Buddha had to say about the dangers of liquor."

I explained to Anup that in the *Sigalovada Sutta,* there are six kinds of dangers related to alcohol addition. They are:[1]

Loss of wealth. It was easy for me to explain this, as Anup had lost a fortune, which was his family inheritance. He had also lost his house, career, wife, and only child.

Increase in quarrels. Quarrels led to domestic violence in Anup's life. He even tried to involve me, a monk, in quarrels using verbal abuse. Alcoholics often abuse their own children, many of whom repeat the cycle and abuse *their* children.

Ill health. Alcohol affects both the physical and mental health of a person. In extreme cases, such as Anup's, alcoholics may experience psychotic symptoms, including hallucinations, as they attempt to withdraw from alcohol. Alcoholism may result in loss of memory and permanent damage to brain cells and the central nervous system. It can also damage the muscles of the heart and eventually cause heart failure.

Loss of reputation. After a while, an alcoholic loses credibility with friends and associates and eventually develops the reputation of one who is not to be trusted.

Indecent exposure. Alcoholics are often not aware of their actions. Sometimes they will say things and expose themselves in other inappropriate ways, which causes embarrassment to the observers.

Impairment of intelligence. When one is under the influence of alcohol, one is sometimes unable to define right from wrong and cannot make sensible decisions. One often makes a fool of oneself in society.

After I finished explaining these teachings of the Buddha to Anup, an Indian parable occurred to me that I felt I should share with him. It goes like this.

Once there was an ascetic meditating in the forest of India. A woman approached him carrying a baby goat, a knife, and a gourd containing liquor. She told the ascetic that he had three options, which were

> To kill the goat, roast it, and eat with her
> To have a sexual relationship with her
> To drink alcohol with her

Then she told the ascetic that if he didn't select one of these options she would kill him and then kill herself. The ascetic was in a quandary because all three options were against his principles. He presumed that the lesser evil would be alcohol. Therefore, he drank with her, got intoxicated, killed and enjoyed the goat, and had a relationship with her!

I further explained to Anup how over twenty-five hundred years ago, the Buddha had preached to all Buddhists to abstain from alcohol. These messages helped to convince Anup that he should use his will power to its fullest extent, that he must be determined to develop the right effort to embark on his new, sober life and make amends for his past. Finally, I quoted the Buddha's words in the Dhammapada:

> He who by good deeds covers the evil he has done, illuminates this world like the moon freed from clouds.[2]

SEVENTEEN

Painful Consequences

Panno, an American monk ordained in Thailand, was expected to arrive shortly in Los Angeles. His teacher in Bangkok had called and asked me to receive him. I thought it would be appropriate for his sister Cathy to welcome him, so I called her and asked her to pick him up at the airport.

They came to my Vihara directly from Los Angeles International Airport and I was very happy to see such a well-disciplined monk before me. His gait was steady, slow, and determined. His speech was soft and accurate. He had a peaceful countenance, which pleased me. Cathy, on the other hand, looked sad and disappointed. While her brother was engaged talking to the other monks, she took me aside and asked if she could have a few words with me in private. Later, when Panno was unpacking in the guest room, she came up to my office.

"Bob, or Panno, as you call him, seems very strange to me now, Bhante," Cathy complained.

"What do you mean, Cathy?" I asked.

"My brother seems very cold," she responded. "He has

no emotion. I haven't seen him in five years, but he never even allowed me to hug him. In fact, he even refused to sit next to me in the car. I felt like a chauffeur."

"Cathy, let me explain that your brother has just returned after five years of rigid, celibate, monastic training. In the Theravada tradition, monks are not allowed to have physical contact with females, even their mothers or sisters. His behavior is normal for a monk, but even monks need to realize that they have to adapt to the context in which they live. In Theravadan countries, when a female drives, monks do not sit in the front seat. However, in the Western world, if you do not sit with the driver, it is an insult. I am positive that as time goes by, he will be more flexible in his thinking."

I noticed that Cathy was still uneasy, perhaps even a bit angry, so I allowed her to talk.

"Bhante," she began, "I hope Bob will continue to treat me like a sister. I can't understand, though, that with all his strict discipline, he still seems to be smoking. I couldn't help but smell the odor, and I had hoped that he had finally quit."

I made no comment about Panno and his smoking, and Cathy bid me good-bye.

A few days later I was feeding the pigeons on the sidewalk when Panno approached me. He told me about his strict monastic training in Sing Buri, which lies in the outskirts of Bangkok. While we were talking, two young American men who were walking by stopped and stared at us. They were curious to know who we were.

While we were having a friendly conversation, Panno slipped away. I felt uneasy and looked around. Much to my disappointment, standing there near the house was Panno, smoking, his back to the three of us. The two visitors eventually continued on their way, and Panno stepped up, eager to know what we had been talking about.

Instantly I replied, "They were talking about you."

"What about me?" he asked, surprised.

"Well, they seem perplexed to see a monk smoking. They questioned whether Buddhist monks are allowed to smoke."

"Bhante, what did you say?"

"I replied that monks must not smoke, as it is against the teachings of the Buddha."

"Why did you let me down?" he asked, sadly.

"I did not let you down, Panno. I explained the Buddha's teaching."

"Bhante, in Thailand some monks smoke, and lay devotees even offer them cigarettes. This is a common practice. In fact, in the Vinaya I found out that the Buddha himself had allowed monks to smoke."

"Panno, I know what you are talking about. In the *Vinaya Pitaka* the Buddha permitted the monks to inhale the vapor from herbal concoctions. This could be done only if they were sick, to give them relief. There was no mention of tobacco in this medicinal remedy."

"Bhante, you strongly say that smoking is against Buddha's teachings. Can you support your statement?" he asked challengingly.

"Of course. In the Middle Length Sayings, chapter 61, the Buddha advised his son Rahula this way, 'You should reflect upon that same bodily action thusly: Does this action that I am doing with the body lead to my own affliction, or to the affliction of others, or to the affliction of both? If it is an unwholesome bodily action with painful consequences, with painful results, then you should suspend such bodily action.'"[1]

"Panno, I would like to further explain why I think that smoking is against the Buddha's teaching. The American Cancer Society estimates that over four hundred thousand deaths occur annually due to smoking. Also, smokers are at increased risk for cancer of the larynx, oral cavity, esophagus, bladder, kidneys, and pancreas. Smoking causes a fivefold increase in the risk of dying from chronic bronchitis, and emphysema. Cigar and pipe smoke contain the same toxic and carcinogenic compounds found in cigarette smoke.

"Therefore, when you smoke, you are deliberately destroying yourself. This, according to the Buddha, is an unwholesome act.

"In addition, recent research has focused on the effects of environmental tobacco smoke, the effect of tobacco smoke on nonsmokers who must share the same environment. It states that exposure to secondhand smoke, which contains all the toxic agents inhaled by a smoker, causes cancer and can aggravate asthma, pneumonia, and bronchitis, and can impair blood circulation. It emphasizes that regular exposure to secondhand smoke almost doubles the risk of heart disease.

"A smoker doubles his unwholesome actions because he destroys himself as well as others. Unfortunately, even unborn babies, children, and other innocent people are affected by secondhand smoke."

"Bhante," Panno replied, "I want to stop smoking. Tell me how I can get over this destructive habit."

"Panno, in the same chapter, the Buddha explained to Rahula how to overcome bad habits. He said, 'Then, you should confess such a bodily action, reveal it, and lay it upon the teacher or your wise companion in the holy life. Having confessed it, revealed it, and laid it open, you should undertake restraint for the future.'

"According to the Buddhist way of training, emancipation is a gradual process. It cannot be done overnight unless you have a strong determination. As an example, when you learn swimming, you start at the shallow end. Then gradually you learn to swim in the deeper end. You definitely do not plunge into the deep end first.

"Panno, how many cigarettes do you smoke each day?"

"Two packets, Bhante."

"When you sleep tonight, make a firm decision that you will smoke only thirty-nine cigarettes, not forty, tomorrow. Take out the first cigarette and put it in the trash can. The second night, before you go to sleep, appreciate your willpower and continue the same technique by reducing your cigarette consumption by two. The third day, reduce by three. In this manner you will be able to get over your habit within forty days. I am positive you will be proving your willpower as well.

"We, as Buddhist monks, must be mindful of every movement of our body, speech, and mind. We are the expounders of the doctrine of the Buddha. The Buddhist monks are the role models of the followers of Buddhism. We are the cynosure of the society; therefore, our lives must be exemplary.

"I recall a Jataka parable wherein a bodhisattva was admonished by an angel. The bodhisattva was taking a bath in a lake. He saw a beautiful lotus blossom near him, and without cutting it, he lifted it up to his face to enjoy its fragrance. This innocent action somehow annoyed an angel who was watching nearby. She reprimanded the bodhisattva for polluting the flower. Meanwhile, in the same lake, a man had bathed, plucked lotuses, and pulled up the roots. The bodhisattva asked the angel why his innocent act was questioned, while the man who destroyed the lotuses was not blamed. The angel replied that on a white cloth if there is a spot, it is easily visible. On a dark cloth, if there is a spot, it is invisible. Therefore, people who are held in high esteem by the society are expected to maintain their wholesomeness."[2]

Panno held up his hands in a *wai*, the Thai sign of respect, and said, "Bhante, you have made me realize that I have to seriously clean up not only my act, but my unwholesome habit as well. I will abide by the program you suggested, but I will eliminate *three* cigarettes per day."

Panno did, in fact, quit smoking as he had promised, and he speaks against it strongly even today.

The Dhammapada says,

> By effort, by vigilance, by restraint, by control, let the wise man make for himself an island which the flood cannot overwhelm.[3]

EIGHTEEN

The Sunbather

People often wonder about the life of a monk, especially one such as me, who was ordained as a twelve-year-old child. I often find that devotees wish to prevent me from seeing things that might shock or embarrass me. I appreciate their caring attitude, but I also must say that monks, like all people, must face reality in whatever form it shows itself. However, I am quite sure that the desire to protect me was the underlying cause of an amusing set of circumstances on a hot summer afternoon in the desert in 1979.

As was his habit, Ron leaned over his desk at the office, as if balancing on a soapbox, right before asking me to do something for him.

"Bhante," he said in a long draw of breath, "would you be willing to teach a group of us during a retreat this coming weekend?"

I was always happy to teach, but I wanted to know all the details. "Tell me about it, Ron, and I'll decide," I replied. Ron often got me involved in things that I might have said no to, had I been given the complete story.

"Well, it's about ten of us, and we're going to go up to Mojave to fast. It will mostly be new meditators. Are you game?"

I wasn't exactly sure what he meant by "game," but certainly if they were learning about Buddhism and fasting, they definitely wouldn't be hunting wild animals. I figured I was safe in that respect. "I'll be glad to go, Ron. It sounds all right to me. But I'm not sure about the fasting. I think I'd rather just eat moderately, if that's OK," I responded.

"OK with me, Bhante. I'll pick you up on Friday around 10:00 A.M.," Ron said as he jumped up and dashed out the door.

Retreats. Weekend fixers. Trees take time to grow, and so do their cousins: people. Perceptions can change in a weekend, but that's not consciousness. Drugs can also change perception, but never consciousness. Changing consciousness is a matter of enrichment and experience over time, not merely the altering of perceptions or points of view, which can change with every passing second. I thought about our actions, the things we actually do as human beings, and how they create what winds up being the results or consequences of our lives. Our combined experiences are eventually distilled into understanding, and understanding eventually births vision and enlightenment. That's more than a weekend retreat can do, but I always feel that perhaps a seed can be planted at a retreat that might in time grow into a tree. These were my thoughts about the value of retreats before we set out for the desert.

Ron arrived Friday at 10:00 A.M. Joining us on the journey was a young American monk named Bill, who was recently ordained in Thailand. We packed up the car and took off.

The trip in midsummer was unbearably hot, even for a Sri Lankan. Everyone came outside to meet us when we arrived. There were about twelve people who approached me as I got out of Ron's car, and they all introduced themselves to me. They seemed like a nice bunch of young people, and they all indicated that they were very keen to practice meditation.

As I approached the solitary house, which seemed to be miles from its nearest neighbor, I noticed that it was surrounded by huge rocks, cacti, and acres of desert sand. When I went inside, I got the feeling that the house wasn't as clean as it probably would have been if it were a permanent dwelling for a family, rather than just a weekend rental.

We sat down in the living room and discussed the schedule for the retreat. Afterward, everyone went their own way to complete their final round of cleaning and setting up, and then we had a short rest. As scheduled, I began chanting in Pali around 6:00 P.M., and then we meditated for two hours. After a short *dhamma* talk, and since it was late and everyone was exhausted, we all headed for bed. I don't, however, think I was the only hungry one. We hadn't stopped for food during our trip.

The next morning we began our meditation at dawn. Since the group was fasting, there wasn't a breakfast, and as the morning drew on, I was really getting hungry. At the eleven o'clock break I asked Bill if he could prepare something for me to eat before noon.

"Of course" he replied, "but you must not go outside. And don't look out the windows either, OK? Don't ask me why. Just stay here and I'll fix something for you to eat. What did you have in mind? There's fruit, some rice . . ." Bill continued to rattle off a list of available luncheon items, but my mind wandered in another direction. I thought, Why can't I go outside? What's going on? It was a real curiosity. I can't look out the windows? Something good? Something bad? Something's definitely going on, that much I knew.

". . . And Bhante, it looks like there's some cabbage, and here's a tomato," Bill said, as he continued to run off the menu possibilities. I pretended to be listening, but actually I was becoming very curious.

"Bill, I'm going to the bathroom. Be back in a minute, OK? Just fix me anything. I'm so hungry, it doesn't matter."

I went to the bathroom and slowly slid the window open. It was over the toilet, so I closed the lid and stood on the seat to get a better view. Determined to find out just what was going on, I got an unexpected eyeful! There in the yard, in full and plain view, lay a sunbather—completely nude. It was one of the meditators, a woman. I quickly closed the window and quietly hopped down off the toilet. No wonder Bill insisted that I not go outside.

I opened the bathroom door and walked back into the kitchen, all this taking only a few moments. Bill wouldn't even look up at me as he busily fixed my lunch. His face was bright red, but whenever I spoke to him he responded only "yes" or "no." As soon as he finished fixing my lunch, he hurried out of the room. I thought that maybe I should have taken more time in the bathroom. In fact, I realized he probably knew what I'd been up to when I remembered I didn't even "fake" my visit by flushing the toilet.

The next session started at 2:00 P.M. Bill started to give a lecture with a raging, thunderous voice. He shouted, "Friends! Your behavior is shameful! You must understand, things are very different in Asia than they are in America. The Theravada tradition is different from Western religious systems. The monks come to this country, but they don't know anything! Especially Bhante Piyananda. He became a monk when he was only twelve years old. He has no experience, from a worldly perspective. You had better behave yourselves. I warn you all! Nude sunbathing is not allowed here!"

As he spoke I knew the cat was out of the bag, and no

one was in the dark about what was going on. Ron broke the silence and stood up to apologize. "Bhante, on behalf of everyone present, I'm sorry about this embarrassing situation. We never intended for you to break your precept, or to humiliate you. Please forgive us."

Bill rocked back and forth as if to find his center of balance, nodding silently.

"Well," I said, "as you know, we have been practicing awareness here at the retreat." The group smiled in agreement. I think they were relieved to sense that I was not upset. "So, as we watch our breath arising and falling, we become aware of the rising and falling of all things. This stage of insight is known as *vipassana*."

Everyone seemed to be wondering where I was going with my talk. I proceeded, "As we continue our practice, we become more aware of what is going on inside our bodies. Then we slowly see our bodies as neither a permanent entity, nor as a person. We see how different phenomena rise and fall, that our bodies, even our cells, are constantly in movement and change. We therefore do not become attached to anything. Our craving eventually is transformed into understanding and awareness. The impermanence of the body is completely realized, as is the creation and destruction of all things."

Diane spoke up and said, "Bhante, what you say makes perfect sense. The concept of impermanence, that's a big one. Could you expand on this, and tell us about the elements and how they relate to the idea of impermanence?"

I was impressed by this girl's question, so I paused a moment to focus before responding. "Life is basically expressed through five elements: earth, water, fire, wind, and space. The head, hair, nails, skin, flesh, teeth, sinews, bones, bone marrow, and organs are the elements of earth. All of these, and other bodily parts that are solid in nature, are designated as elements of earth. As for water, any bodily component that is fluid in nature would be designated water. The element of fire is of the nature of heat within the body. This is provided by what we eat, drink, chew, or taste. Also, anything else in the body that has a heating characteristic is designated as the fire element. As for wind, this element embraces the characteristic of the upward and downward flow of air. Finally there is another element, which is called space. This is present in all the empty spaces and cavities of the body."[1]

Bill raised his hand, as did the others. I called on Bill because I could see that he was particularly eager to ask his question. "Bhante, how do these five elements relate to attachments? Can you answer this in terms of attachment to a particular craving or person?"

"Well," I continued, "it is true that people become attached to each other. Mothers and fathers become attached to their children. Children become attached to their parents. And in other relationships, such as a man to a woman, or a woman to a man, it is quite normal for them to become attached to each other. But when we examine our bodies, as we separate all the elements—the earth, the fire, the water, the wind, and the space—we see beyond our bodies to a deeper understanding of ourselves.

"We begin to realize that our bodies are constantly moving in a kind of cosmic dance. Then those concepts that underlie the definition of 'me and mine' completely dissolve and we see 'emptiness' as the activity that is really occurring, in all its immensity and beauty. At this point we are then nothing and free to roam anywhere in the cosmos, without the illusion of craving. We are able to go where we are led to go, to love each being unconditionally, and to move within our universe as we please. These ideas are expressed by scientists nowadays in a multitude of scientific perspectives such as those in quantum physics."

A timid voice arose in the room, which had become

quiet, the group deep in thought about what I had just said. "Bhante, do you have a meditation that would develop the kind of insight you speak of? Could you share any ideas that might help us to see these awarenesses?"

I responded, "Sure."

"Please show us!" another voice piped up, excited with expectation.

"I will teach you a technique that involves concentration on your inhalations and exhalations. While you are practicing this, look into your body and begin to remove each element from your body, one at a time. Take out all the earth, and then the wind, and then the water, and then the fire. When you have visualized the disposal of all these elements, then you will see that what is left over is nothing more than empty space. Also, you can do the same meditation by removing all the elements of your persona, such as your job, where you are from, your relationships with others, and in general, all of those kinds of labels and ego definitions. You will eventually begin to understand, in the universal sense, that you are undefined, empty, and totally free.

"So, my friends, attachment to things, to definitions such as, 'I'm only the body, I'm only this or that, or you are only this or that' are based on nothing but ego. They are the illusions that limit us. In actuality, we are, in our true nature, undefined and unlimited."

There was a deep, warm silence in the meditation hall. Smiles on the faces of the twelve individuals showed me that their hearts were beginning to open.

A young woman raised her hand. "Thank you, Bhante, for showing us the bigger picture. If you would, please tell us a story that might deepen our feelings, that might guide us to this way of seeing?"

I paused for a moment to think of a story that would fit the mood. "I would be happy to tell you this story, which is perhaps two thousand years old and is from Sri Lanka. I think it may help you understand more clearly."

"Please," she responded eagerly.

I continued, "Maha-Tissa Thera, who lived in Mihintale, had cultivated the habit of seeing human bodies as only structures of bones. There are so many techniques of meditation, and this one focuses on impurity. This does not mean that we should not care for and honor our bodies, it's just that Maha-Tissa was, in particular, developing awareness of the impermanence and impurity of the body. This practice is called *atthikasanna*. Do you understand so far?"

The group members nodded quietly and leaned closer, listening carefully.

I continued, "Maha-Tissa was walking one morning and passed a woman who was dressed beautifully, like a goddess. She had just left her house after a quarrel with her husband and was in perverse mood. Upon seeing the *thera* she laughed aloud in a strange way, showing her teeth. Maha-Tissa, upon seeing this strange laugh, noticed her teeth, and the idea of the impurity of the body immediately came to his mind. He had seen the teeth and thought of a skeleton! It is said that he attained arahatship at that very instant. A little later, her husband came upon the road, looking for his wife. When he saw Maha-Tissa he asked him if he had seen a beautiful woman going that way. Maha-Tissa replied that he had only seen a skeleton going along the road."[2]

Everyone in the room laughed.

"There is a another beautiful story in the Dhammapada. Once, there lived in Rajagriha a very beautiful courtesan by the name of Sirima. Every day she offered alms food to the monks, or *bhikkhus*. One of these *bhikkhus* happened to mention to other *bhikkhus* how beautiful Sirima was, and also that she offered very delicious food. On hearing this, a young *bhikkhu* fell in love with Sirima, even without seeing her. The next day, the young *bhikkhu* went with the other *bhikkhus* to the house of Sirima. She was not well on that day, but since she wanted to pay respects to the *bhikkhus*, she was carried to their presence. The young *bhikkhu*, seeing Sirima, thought to himself, Even though she is sick, she is very beautiful, and he developed a strong desire for her.

"That very night, Sirima died. King Bimbisara visited the Buddha and mentioned that Sirima had passed away. The Buddha advised the king to keep the dead body for three days without burying it. By the fourth day, the body of Sirima was no longer beautiful or desirable; it had become bloated and full of maggots. On that day, the Buddha took his *bhikkhus* to the cemetery to observe the dead body. The young *bhikkhu* who was so desperately in love with Sirima did not know that Sirima had died. When he heard that the Buddha and the *bhikkhus* were going to see Sirima, he eagerly joined them. The Buddha then told the king to announce that Sirima would be available for a night, for the payment of one thousand pieces of gold. But nobody would take her for one thousand, or for five hundred, or for two hundred and fifty, or even if she were to be given free of charge. Then the Buddha said to the audience, 'Bhikkhus! Look at Sirima. When she was living, there were many who were willing to give one thousand gold coins to spend one night with her; but now no one will take her, even if given without any payment. The body of a person is subject to deterioration and decay.' After listening to the Buddha, the young monk who had developed his attachment to Sirima realized the real nature of life.[3]

"Therefore my friends, we shouldn't be fooled by appearances. We must learn to understand the impermanent nature of life. We must not be overly attracted by, or attached to, things that please our eyes. We should also not be fearful and run away from unpleasant sights.

"Look at these flowers you have offered at the altar. They

are fresh, fragile, fragrant, and beautiful. In a few days they will wilt and you will discard them, as they will have lost their beauty and be of no use."

I paused for a moment and let them reflect on impermanence. Then I said, "I look now at Bill's face, and I can see the effect that the realization of impermanence has had on him. Earlier today he was red and fuming with anger. Look at him now. He is calm and contented. Now, do you see how impermanent one's own *feelings* are?"

That ended the evening's talk, and the group paid their sincere respects to me and thanked me profusely.

I myself was now in a quiet mood and wanted to be alone for a while. I walked outside to the once "prohibited" area and gazed around me. The gentle breeze made the dry bushes sway, and the sun was gloriously setting, giving the desert a warm saffron glow.

I smiled to myself and savored the experience I had just had with my young American group. With great appreciation for another day of my life in this country, I recalled the following verse:

> Desiring nothing, doubting nothing,
> Beyond judgment and sorrow
> And the pleasures of the senses.
> He has moved beyond time.
> He is pure and free.[4]

NINETEEN

Appearances Are Deceiving

We, as human beings, tend to form opinions about others by looking at the outward appearance and not by getting to know them or by trying to understand their circumstances. I often feel that the people who are most judged by their "image" are celebrities and members of the clergy.

Nikom, a Thai Buddhist monk in his mid-thirties, was a frequent visitor to my temple. He respected my opinion and brought Thai devotees to seek my advice.

One day Nikom came alone with a perturbed expression on his face that instantly told me he needed my guidance. He followed me to my office where we could talk in private.

"Bhante, my mind is in a turmoil," he exclaimed. "I need someone to talk to."

"Nikom, please make yourself comfortable and tell me what happened."

"Bhante, a few weeks ago a Thai devotee came to seek advice from my abbot. It was late in the evening and she had parked her car on the street. When she was ready to leave, the abbot told me to walk her to her car, which was only one block away. Can you imagine? In just that short distance, a Thai couple passing by saw us walking together and told everyone in the community that I was involved with a woman. Their slandering, lashing tongues have completely humiliated me. I feel so ashamed about this rumor that I want to disrobe." Nikom was so upset that he put his face in his hands and wept. Such slander is absolutely the worst form of shame for a Buddhist monk.

I felt generally sorry for the man and searched for words that could help him through this difficult moment. "Nikom, I am surprised at your immaturity," I began. "This sort of gossip is nothing new. We, as monks, must be prepared to face these unfounded charges of misconduct. I have been in your shoes not once, but many times."

"Bhante, you?" he asked, incredulous.

"Yes, Nikom. What I am about to tell you is my own experience." Then I told him the following story.

It was in 1983 that I was called upon by our ambassador to conduct the funeral service of a Sri Lankan monk in Hawaii. After the service, a fellow Sri Lankan offered to take me to see my friend, a Thai monk who was at that time living in Honolulu. His name was Pradeep, and he was a smiling, jovial man whose English was limited to words of endearment only.

Pradeep was a visiting monk at Wat Thai in Chicago when I was at Northwestern University. When I called him to say I was in Hawaii he was delighted to welcome me to his temple, and we spent some very enjoyable time reminiscing about our Chicago days. He arranged for me to see the island with his friend, Mr. Shin. After completing the "circle island tour" he dropped me off at Ala Moana Shopping Center, saying that he would return for me in two hours. He had some errands to run.

While I was walking through the central courtyard of the mall, a group of teenagers approached me. They made joking, but polite, remarks about my yellow robe, and they gathered around me, asking questions about where I was from.

Before I knew what was happening, in a split second, one boy had snatched my bag and disappeared into the afternoon crowd. The rest of the boys ran after him, never looking back.

I was shocked. All my belongings, including my green card, air ticket, and cash, were gone. I found a security officer, told him my story, and then made a formal report to the police officers who were called to the scene. Then I returned to Pradeep's temple in a taxicab.

My old friend paid the taxi driver and then patiently listened to my anguished tale of woe. When I was finished explaining, I was surprised when Pradeep laughed and said, "Good for you!"

He took the situation into his very competent hands, and within a couple of days, he got me a new air ticket and gave me some cash so I could return home to Los Angeles.

A couple of months after my trip to Hawaii, the Sri Lankan man who had driven me around the island stopped by to visit Pradeep. Pradeep very flippantly told my friend Buddhi, "Oh, Bhante Piyananda had good time in Honolulu. Girl came, took bag, no money, no ticket, everything gone." He said this in a very laughing, joking manner.

"Tell me what happened to Ven. Piyananda," Buddhi replied, genuinely concerned. He had not heard about my misadventure at Ala Moana Center.

"Waikiki gone, shopping mall lady came took bag sweetheart." As I said, Pradeep's English was not very good at that time.

Pradeep's story caused Buddhi to become suspicious about me.

Later on, Buddhi called his friend Ari, in Los Angeles, and told him that Ven. Piyananda had gone to Waikiki where a girl had snatched his bag. After the story got told a few times, it grew more and more interesting, the details getting spicier and spicier. Eventually it was said that Ven. Piyananda had put on a pair of shorts and a flowered aloha shirt and had gone with a bunch of girls down to Waikiki Beach. The girls got him drunk on Mai Tais at the Royal Hawaiian and stole his bag!

The disparaging comments turned the molehill into a mountain, and the false rumor about me caused a division in the Sri Lankan community. My sincere friends who knew me well were absolutely certain that such a story could never be true. On the other hand, those individuals who enjoyed a good gossip were sure I had broken my precepts.

"How did you solve the problem, Bhante?" asked Nikom, who by this time had completely forgotten his own problem.

"My spiritual advisor and our senior monk, Ven. Dr. Ratanasara, had gotten wind of this false report about me. He never questioned me about the incident, because he trusted me implicitly, even though he felt very bad to hear the rumors.

"Three months later, however, when he returned from Hawaii after a conference, he called me to his room and told me that he had gotten firsthand information about the unfortunate episode. He said that he had gone to the Thai temple accompanied by Buddhi to speak to Pradeep. He asked to speak to the person who had taken me to Ala Moana Center, and a few minutes later Mr. Shin appeared. Mr. Shin explained exactly what had happened, and Ven. Dr. Ratanasara then realized that it was Pradeep's limited command of English—combined with his joking, but endearing, words—that had led to the misunderstanding. He told Pradeep to perfect his English and be careful how he used it; he pointed out the damage that he had innocently caused me."

"Bhante," said Nikom, "I remember the Buddha telling

his followers not to relate exactly what one has seen. What did he mean by that?"

"Nikom, I believe that what you are referring to is in the *Anguttara Nikaya,* when he advised Vassakara, the Brahmin."

"Bhante, could you please explain this *sutta* to me?" asked Nikom.

"Vassakara was having a discussion with the Buddha about communicating the truth. In the course of their conversation Vassakara said that he would tell exactly what he sees, relate exactly what he hears, speak exactly what he senses, and say exactly what he realizes.

"The Buddha answered by saying, 'Vassakara, if you see anything, hear anything, sense anything, or realize anything that might be harmful to yourself or to others, do not repeat it.'"[1]

"I suppose, as Buddhist monks, we have to be more mindful of our actions than lay people, yes?" asked Nikom.

"Absolutely. Do you remember Manikara Kubupaga Tissa's story in the Dhammapada?"

"Not really, Bhante."

Here is the famous story as I related it to Nikom.

The monk Tissa was friendly with a goldsmith. While the other monks went from door to door collecting alms, Tissa was invited by his friend, who prepared alms for him.

This goldsmith was a royal jeweler. One day while he was cutting meat for the midday meal, Tissa arrived and sat in his kitchen, where there was a pet eagle sitting on his perch. At that very moment a messenger delivered a precious stone to the goldsmith to be faceted. The goldsmith accepted it with a bloody hand and put it down on the kitchen table. After cutting the meat, he covered it up with a cloth and went to wash his hands.

When the goldsmith returned, he noticed at once that the precious stone was gone. He questioned his wife, searched all over the house, and turned to the monk. "Did you take the precious stone, venerable monk?"

"No, I did not," replied Tissa.

"What happened to it then?" he asked angrily. "There was no one else around. You were the only one in the room."

The monk remained silent. The goldsmith became fearful for his life, because the stone had come from the royal palace. The punishment for losing or stealing such a stone would certainly mean his death. He went into a furious rage, then hit and tied up the monk, threatening to kill him if he did not admit to the theft.

The monk was bleeding profusely from the vicious beating. Then, seeing the blood, the eagle came to drink it. This made the goldsmith even angrier, and he dashed the bird to the ground.

The monk begged the goldsmith to see whether the bird was dead or alive. When he realized the bird was dead, he told the goldsmith to examine the contents of its stomach. To the embarrassment of the goldsmith, the precious, missing gemstone was right there inside the poor dead animal.

The monk softly whispered, "I saw the bird swallow the stone covered with blood. I did not tell you because I was afraid you would take its life. As a monk, even if I am a witness to an incident, I cannot report it if it causes a life to be taken."[2]

Nikom pondered what I had told him and then said, "Bhante, I can tolerate onlookers reporting what they have seen, but not the unfounded gossip they spread."

"Nikom, let me tell you another story." I could tell that the young monk was still upset.

"There was a teacher who was practicing meditation with his pupils. After one session, the teacher looked at one of his students and remarked, 'While you were meditating I looked at your face. You seemed peaceful, calm, and serene, like a buddha.'

"The young man laughed and replied, 'Sir, I, too, saw you while you were meditating. You appeared like an old, dirty pig seated on a pile of cow dung.'

"The other pupils got angry over this remark, but the teacher calmed them by these words. 'My mind is pure and clean like a buddha's. Therefore, I saw this student as a buddha. Unfortunately, this poor young man's mind is dirty and polluted. That is why he saw me like an old pig. If you wear red glasses, everything you perceive will appear to be red. If you wear green glasses, everything will be green. People are neither red nor green. It is the glasses one wears that create the illusion.'"

"Bhante, I understand the meaning of your story," Nikom replied. "Yet, I still have fears about my acceptance by the community. I am afraid they will believe the gossip about me rather than the truth."

"Don't worry, Nikom. Even the Buddha was faced with more acute problems than yours. He did not run away from them. He faced them squarely."

"I cannot recall such an incident among the stories of the Buddha's life," remarked Nikom.

I then proceeded to tell him this true story.

The disbelievers of the Buddha, a group of heretics, plotted to disgrace and slander the Buddha. They hired Sundari, a prostitute, to pretend to the community that she had spent the night in the monastery where the Buddha was staying. She actually spent the night in a neighboring house and in the morning returned from the direction of the monastery.

After a few days, these heretics hired villains to kill Sundari and hide her body under a heap of rubbish. They spread the rumor that Sundari was missing. Later, when the body was found, they carried it through the streets, blaming her death on the Buddha and his followers. As a result, the monks were insulted, ignored, and physically abused. The people stopped giving them alms.

Then Ananda, the Buddha's attendant, suggested to the Buddha that they leave the city. The Buddha said, "Ananda, what if the people of the next city we visit start treating us the same way?"

"Venerable Sir," replied Ananda, "then we'll go to yet another city."

"If we receive the same treatment there, then what shall we do? Ananda, we should never run away from a problem. We must face problems like an elephant that is trained to face a sheath of arrows flying toward him from all directions. The truth will always surface regardless of the amount of time that passes. Don't worry, no one can harm the reputation of a buddha for more than seven days."[3]

In exactly seven days the heretics who plotted and killed Sundari were brought to justice.

"Finally, Nikom, I want to share with you a quote from the Dhammapada. 'It is not new, O Atula! It has always been done from ancient times. They blame one who is silent, they blame one who speaks much, and they blame one who speaks little. There is no one in this world who is not blamed. There never has been, there never will be, nor is there now, anyone who is always blamed or always praised.'"[4]

Nikom showed signs of relief as he left my temple. I was glad that I could convince him to remain a monk.

TWENTY

The Seven Types
of Wealth

Peter was in his late teens when I met him in 1976 on Holly-wood Boulevard near my favorite bookstore. He approached me and asked whether I was a Buddhist monk. When I replied in the affirmative he was delighted.

"Wow! I've been looking for a Buddhist monk for a number of years."

"Is there any particular reason that you are looking for a Buddhist monk?" I asked.

"Man, I am a Buddhist, too."

"Are your parents Buddhists?"

"No way. They are definitely not Buddhists," he replied with a laugh.

Then I asked him how he became interested in Buddhism. In response, he told me an astonishing story of an incident that had occurred when he was a five-year-old child.

His parents took him on vacation to Tijuana, Mexico. While walking on the roadside they saw many kinds of ceramic figurines for sale. All of a sudden Peter became fascinated by a particular statue and told his parents he wanted it. His father reprimanded him, saying that it was a statue of the Buddha, and he couldn't have it. Peter cried in protest, demanding that they buy the ceramic figure for him, but his parents paid no heed. They got into their car and crossed the border, but Peter's crying did not stop.

Finally his mother got tired of listening to her screaming little boy and suggested to her husband that they return to Tijuana and buy the statue. This they did, and Peter was delighted that he was able to get it. When they got home, he placed it in a prominent place in his bedroom because he felt some sort of unexplained connection with it.

That night before bedtime, he said, "Mommy, can you tell me more about the Buddha?"

"I'm sorry, Peter, but I really don't know very much about him at all. We're Jewish. I'll go to the library in the morning and do some research. Maybe I can tell you more at bedtime tomorrow."

Peter smiled, happy to hear this news.

The following night Peter's mother tucked him in bed and began the story of the Buddha that she had learned earlier that day.

"The Buddha was a great and compassionate man who lived in India twenty-five hundred years ago, Peter. He was born a prince, and all during his youth he enjoyed a happy, blessed life, and he was given everything he ever wanted. Later he got married to the girl his parents picked out for him, and they had a baby son. Throughout his whole life, he never saw anything that was unpleasant or unhappy, until one day he went outside his father's palace walls and saw an old man, a sick man, the body of a dead man, and a poor holy man. He didn't understand what he had seen, and for a long time he thought about why people went through life suffering."

"Mommy, am I going to get old and sick one day, too?" asked Peter innocently.

"I'm afraid everyone gets old, Peter, but I hope you don't get sick," she replied.

Peter tried to understand his mother's words, but at the time he couldn't imagine what it would be like to be old and suffering.

His mother continued. "At the age of twenty-nine the young prince left the palace and decided to search for the truth. Prince Siddhartha, as he was called, gave up his royal clothes, put on a simple robe, and went to the forest to meditate."

"What's meditation, Mommy?" asked Peter.

"I'm not too sure about it, son, but I think it's being real quiet, maybe a kind of praying."

"So what did he do then?"

"After six years of trying many different kinds of practice, Prince Siddhartha went to a place called Gaya and sat under a bodhi tree."

"That's a funny name for a tree, Mommy. Do we have those here?"

"No, Peter, bodhi trees only grow on the other side of the world, in Asia. Maybe one day you can go there and see one."

"So what did he do under the tree, Mommy?" Peter had a serious look on his face that told his mother he really did care about the Buddha.

"Prince Siddhartha made a firm resolution. He said, 'My skin and bones may dry up. My flesh and blood may dry up in my body, but until I attain enlightenment, I will not leave this seat.'"

"Can you tell me what attain enlightenment means?"

By this time Peter's mother was running out of answers as well as patience, trying to explain such difficult things to such a young boy. "I think it means knowing the difference between what is right and what is wrong, Peter, but even more than that. It also means becoming really smart and knowing all the answers."

"Can I become smart and know the answers, too, Mommy?" Peter's face lit up when he asked this question, as if he fully understood that it was possibile.

"Of course you can, Peter. You can become anything in this world you want to be. Do you want me to continue with the story?"

"Oh yes, Mommy. Please tell me what happened under that tree."

"Well, it was on the full moon day in May that Prince Siddhartha attained full enlightenment and all of a sudden knew all of the answers in the world. This is why he is called the 'Buddha,' which means 'All Knowing of the Past, the Present, and the Future.' At that moment the Buddha understood the cause of suffering, which was the question he had asked himself from the beginning. He discovered that when there is suffering, there is a problem that is causing the suffering. He understood that when the cause of the suffering is removed, the suffering disappears.

"After realizing the truth, the Buddha spent seven days looking up at the bodhi tree to show his thanks for the fact that it had given him shelter. He did this to show the world that we must appreciate the people or things that help us.

"For forty-five years the Buddha preached the truth he had learned. He had many followers, both men and women, who gave their lives to practicing his teaching. The Buddha finally passed away when he was eighty years old."

Then Peter had asked his mother whether there were any monks and nuns still living. The mother had replied that she thought there would be.

It was on that day that Peter decided he was a Buddhist.

Many times during the following years, Peter would announce to his family that he was, in fact, a Buddhist. Everyone would smile politely, but no one took him seriously, because he was too young to know what he believed in, or at least, that's what his parents thought. Eventually, however, when Peter was in his early teens, the family could no longer ignore what he said he was, and his father eventually became furious with him because of his belief. He even sometimes blamed his wife, Peter's mother, for exposing the child to Buddhism.

"That is quite a story, Peter," I exclaimed, when he finally finished telling me about his introduction to Buddhism.

I invited him to visit me at the Meditation Center the following day, and during the course of the next three or four months, we became good friends. I gave Peter a number of books about Buddhism, and encouraged him to attend the meditation classes, which he did.

One day after meditation, Peter asked me if he could have a private word with me in my room. The first words that came out of his mouth were, "I want to be ordained a Buddhist monk, Bhante. Will you help me?"

"That is quite a serious step to take, Peter. Are you quite sure about this?" Several times during my stay in the United States I have had young men and women approach me about wanting to enter the *sangha*. I always advise them to be absolutely sure before making such a commitment, which, in my country of Sri Lanka, is for a lifetime.

"I am sure, Bhante, more sure than about anything in my life."

I felt that Peter was sincere, so I took him to the Thai temple with my dear friend Suwat. Peter was ordained immediately, given further training, and sent to Bangkok by the abbot.

I kept in touch with Peter, and one day in 1979 I received a letter from him. By that time he went by the name Saddhajivo. I had known that Peter came from an extremely wealthy family, but I hadn't known that his father continued to object to his being a monk. Peter said in his letter that his father had finally decided to disinherit him if he did not give up his robe.

Peter said that he truly loved his parents. He also said that he, too, had the greatest wealth in the world: his robe and his alms bowl.

I immediately replied to his letter, stating that I admired his decision not to disrobe. I said, "When practicing Buddhism, the Buddha told us that a person acquires seven different kinds of wealth, none of which can be destroyed or taken away."[1]

I explained these seven types of wealth in my letter, and I will share them here.

> *Saddha.* This term is generally translated as faith or belief. In fact, the root word, *sad,* means good, and *dha* means holding or keeping fast to one's being. Thus, we can say that *saddha* also means holding good in one's mind. *Saddha,* according to the Buddha's teachings, is rational faith, not *blind* faith. The emphasis here is on confidence, seeing, knowing, and understanding. I said in my letter, "Saddhajivo, your name itself means 'a person who leads a life with confidence, trust, and understanding of Buddhist practice.' You do, in fact, possess this type of wealth."
>
> *Sila.* This translates as virtue or moral conduct, the highest principle of human behavior. *Sila* can be divided into two parts: positive actions and avoidance actions. On the positive side, it dictates that one should discipline the mind, the body, and the speech so that one can contribute responsibly to one's family and society. On the avoidance side, one is given a list of unwholesome actions from which to abstain and is told to avoid allowing unwholesome, negative thoughts from entering one's mind. The

Buddha said that as a virtuous person, one is neither a hindrance to oneself nor an obstacle to others. Virtue, therefore, is a type of wealth that can only be obtained through self-development, self-cultivation, and self-realization.

Hiri. This type of wealth has to do with self-respect, which arises from within when one thinks of saying or doing something that is not wholesome. Contemplating how it would feel to bring disgrace upon oneself, one's parents, or one's family discourages one from carrying out any unwholesome impulse. Self-respect, therefore, keeps us on a positive, pure, and growthful path, which is a part of living rich, full lives.

Ottappa. This type of wealth can be called self-preservation, which leads us to abstain from unwholesome or illegal acts in order to protect our reputation and preserve our freedom. Most people fear the results that would befall us if we were to succumb to the temptation to commit wrongful acts. The Buddha said, "The doer of evil reaps evil results. The doer of goodwill gathers good results." Self-respect and self-preservation work together in our minds and serve as protective shields against our thinking, saying, or doing negative and unwholesome thoughts, words, or deeds. I sometimes liken these guardians of wealth to police patrol cars. Even when we see a patrol car on the other side of the freeway, we tend to slow down.

Suta. This very valuable type of wealth is the wealth of education. With a good education, we are equipped to be able to face and solve any and all problems we are given in life. An education ideally brings out the noble and virtuous qualities in an individual. It helps one to see things as they truly are, to cultivate wholesome habits, and to be able to detect and eliminate any unwholesome habits (this includes negative thought patterns) that might have developed. Education doesn't mean only academic achievements; it also means acquiring wisdom through experience.

Caga. This very beautiful type of wealth is translated as generosity, meaning giving abundantly without expecting anything in return. When one gives, one helps to eliminate craving, the cause of suffering. Being generous makes those with whom we come in contact happy. It also helps the giver be happy. Developing generosity of spirit helps one maintain a pleasant and loving rapport with family members, friends, business associates, and even strangers. Greed, hatred, and delusion are obstacles in the way of our path to enlightenment. The only way to eliminate these roots of destruction is by practicing charity with a generous heart. The practice of charity oftentimes leads one not only to the accumulation of great wealth, but to keeping it as well.

Panna. Perhaps the greatest type of wealth is *panna*, or wisdom. In Buddhist teachings there are actually three types of wisdom: wisdom acquired through experience and education; wisdom acquired through analysis and deductive reasoning; and wisdom acquired through meditation and spiritual insight. The first two types of wisdom are categorized as *nyana*, or knowledge. *Panna* is the third type of wisdom, which is gained only through spiritual practice and deep meditation. *Panna* and ignorance cannot exist in the same human mind. It is through *panna* that we are able to see things in their proper perspective. *Panna* enables us to solve problems, understand the nature of impermanence, and see the underlying influences of causal relations. Ultimately, *panna* enables us to see the interconnectedness of all phenomena, which is the first step toward enlightenment. This is the point at which we realize that there is no self, nothing we can call I or my or mine. All of the obstacles and defilements have been overcome, and the practitioner is on his or her way to attaining *nibbana*. There can be no greater wealth than accumulating *panna*, which leads one to achieving the greatest prize, *nibbana*.

The seven types of wealth as expressed by the Buddha are far more valuable than any kind of worldly wealth we could ever imagine or hope to attain. Saddhajivo has been a monk now for twenty years. Before his father passed away, quite some time ago, Saddhajivo was able to make peace with him and share with him these teachings on the Buddha's seven types of wealth. The father was able to acknowledge that the wealth his son had acquired was far greater than his own.

> Health is the precious gain,
> Contentment the greatest wealth.
> A trustworthy friend is the best relative.
> Nibbana is the highest happiness.[2]

GLOSSARY

AJARN (Thai) Teacher; (Pali) *acariya*

ARAHAT (Pali) One who has perfected himself through the practice of moral conduct, meditation, and wisdom

BHIKKHU (Pali) A Buddhist monk

BODHI TREE The tree under which the ascetic Gautama Siddhartha meditated, and became the Buddha

BODHISATTA (Pali) One who decides to attain enlightenment for the sake of all living beings

BRAHMANS Members of the highest caste in India

CĀGA (Pali) Charity

DANA (Pali) Generosity

DUKKHA (Pali) Suffering; unsatisfactoriness

HIRI (Pali) Self-respect; self-presentation

KARMA (Sanskrit) Intentional actions of mind, speech, and body; (Pali) kamma

KARUNA (Pali) Compassion

METTA (Pali) Loving kindness; universal love

MUDITA (Pali) Sympathetic joy; happiness for others' success

ÑANA (Pali) Knowledge

NIBBANA (Pali) Ultimate reality; calming of all conditioned things; giving up all defilements; detachment; cessation

OTTAPPA (Pali) Moral dread; self-respect

PAHANA (Pali) Removal

PANNA (Pali) Wisdom

PARINIBBANA (Pali) The final passing away of the Buddha or an arahat

PARITTA (Pali) Protection

PINDAOPATA (Pali) Collection of alms

PIRITH (Sinhala) Protection

PEMA (Pali) Affection

RĀGA (Pali) Lust; desire

SADDHĀ (Pali) Confidence; faith; belief

SAMADHI (Pali) Concentration

SANVARA (Pali) Prevention

SATI (Pali) Mindfulness

SILA (Pali) Virtue; morality

SING BURI A Thai province

SINHALESE Primary language of Sri Lanka

SUTA (Pali) Learning; education

SUTTAS (Pali) Discourses; sermons

THERA (Pali) A senior monk with at least ten years since his high ordination

UPEKKHA (Pali) Equanimity

VIRIYA (Pali) Energy

WAI Thai gesture of respect

NOTES

CHAPTER ONE: The Robe

1. E. Hardy, ed., *Suriya Sutta*, in *Anguttara Nikaya*, vol. 4 (London: Pali Text Society, 1958), p. 100.
2. N. K. G. Mendis, *The Questions of King Milinda* (Kandy, Sri Lanka: Buddhist Publication Society, 1993), p. 165.
3. Dr. Henepola Gunaratana, "What Is the Use of Knowledge of Impermanence?" *Dharma Vijaya Journal* (Los Angeles), February 1999.
4. T. W. Rhys-Davis, trans., *Mahavagga, Kandhaka*, in *The Sacred Books of the East* (Delhi: Motilal Banarsidas, 1974), p. 208.
5. *Dhammapada*, v. 10.

CHAPTER TWO: Phoenix Calamity

1. Richard Morris, ed. *Ariyavansa Sutta*, in *Angutttara Nikaya*, vol. 2 (London: Pali Text Society, 1976), p. 27.
2. Dr. Walpola Rahula, "Problems of the Prospects of the Sangha in the West," *Mahabodhi Journal*, April–May 1974.
3. T. W. Rhys-Davis, ed., *Maha Govinda Sutta*, in *Digha Nikaya*, vol. 2 (London: Pali Text Society, 1966), p. 250.
4. *Dhammapada*, v. 5.

CHAPTER THREE: Religious Tolerance

1. Dr. Ananda W. P. Guruge, *Asoka* (Colombo, Sri Lanka: Ministry of Cultural Affairs, 1993), pp. 566–67.
2. N. B. Sen, *Wit and Wisdom of Jawaharlal Nehru* (Delhi: New Book Society of India, 1960), p. 264.
3. Bhikkhu Bodhi, trans., *Majjahima Nikaya, Upali Sutta* (Boston: Wisdom Publications, 1995), p. 477.

4. *Digha Nikaya, Brahmajala Sutta* (Rangoon, Burma: Burma
   Pitaka Association, 1984), p. 5.
5. *Dhammapada*, v. 256, 257.

CHAPTER FOUR: Boundless Compassion

1. *Sutta Nipata, Metta Sutta*, in *Buddha Vandana of Dharma
   Vijaya Buddhist Vihara*, p. 35.

CHAPTER FIVE: The Disciple Who Jumped over the Cliff

1. *Mahaparinibbana Sutta*, in *Digha Nikaya* (Rangoon, Burma:
   Burma Pitaka Association, 1984), p. 5.
2. *Dhammapada*, v. 160.
3. *Dhammapada*, v. 276.
4. Bhikkhu Bodhi, trans., *Vimansaka Sutta*, in *Majjhima
   Nikaya* (Boston: Wisdom Publications, 1995), p. 415.
5. Richard Morris, ed., *Kalama Sutta*, in *Anguttara Nikaya*
   (London: Pali Text Society, 1961), pp. 188–93.
6. Bhikkhu Bodhi, trans., *Alagaduppama Sutta*, in *Majjhima
   Nikaya* (Boston: Wisdom Publications, 1995), p. 224.
7. H. Saddhatissa, trans., *Khaggavisana Sutta*, in *Sutta Nipata*
   (London: Curzon Press, 1987), p. 4.
8. *Dhammapada*, v. 160, 167.

CHAPTER SIX: The Punks Meet the Monk

1. E. Hardy, ed., *Paharada Sutta*, in *Anguttara Nikaya*, vol. 4
   (London: Pali Text Society, 1958), p. 197.
2. Andersen Dines, ed. *Subhasita Sutta Suttanipata*
   (Oxford: Pali Text Society, 1990), pp. 78–79.
3. *Dhammapada*, v. 5.
4. Thera Narada, *The Buddha and His Teachings* (Colombo, Sri
   Lanka: Vajirarama, 1973), chap. 43.
5. *Dhammapada*, v. 36.

CHAPTER SEVEN: The Balancing Act

1. Edward Muller, ed., *Dhammasangani* (London: Pali Text
   Society, 1885), p. 22.

2. Narada Thera, *A Manual of Abhidhamma* (Singapore: Singapore Budddhist Meditation Center, 1989), pp. 87, 93, 304, 332, 337, 344, 361.
3. E. M. Hare, trans., *Sona Sutta*, in *Anguttara Nikaya*, vol. 3 (London: Pali Text Society, 1973), p. 266.
4. *Dhammapada*, v. 166.

CHAPTER EIGHT: Karmic Ties

1. Bhikkhu Nanamoli, *Life of the Buddha* (Kandy, Sri Lanka: Buddhist Publication Society, 1984), pp. 20–29.
2. M. Leon, ed., *Dhammacakkapavattana Sutta*, in *Samyutta Nikaya* (London: Pali Text Society, 1976), pp. 420–24.
3. Dr. Walpola Rahula, *What the Buddha Taught* (London: Gordon Frazer, 1978), p. 16.
4. *Dhammapada*, v. 204.
5. Bhikkhu Bodhi, *The Noble Eightfold Path* (Kandy, Sri Lanka: Buddhist Publication Society, 1984), Wheel Publication No. 308/311.
6. E. Hardy, ed., *Upavana Sutta*, in *Anguttara Nikaya*, vol. 3 (London: Pali Text Society), 1976, p. 195.
7. Ibid., p. 196.
8. M. Leon, ed., *Manibhadda Sutta*, in *Samyutta Nikaya*, vol. 1 (London: Pali Text Society, 1973), p. 208.
9. Ibid., p. 227.
10. K. N. Jayatilleka, *The Message of the Buddha* (New York: Free Press, 1975), pp. 112–18.
11. Robert Chalmers, ed., *Majjhima Nikaya*, vol. 3. *Cullakamma Vibhanga Sutta* (London: Pali Text Society, 1977), pp. 202–6.
12. *Dhammapada*, v. 219–20.

CHAPTER NINE: Detachment—A Way of Life

1. V. Renckner, ed., *Ariyapariyesana Sutta*, in *Majjhima Nikaya*, vol. 1 (London: Pali Text Society, 1979), p. 163.
2. Ibid., *Mahasaccaka Sutta*, p. 240.
3. R. L. Mitra, trans., *Lalitavistara English* (Delhi: Sri Satguru Publications, 1998), pp. 247–48.

4. Thich Nhat Hanh, *Old Path, White Clouds* (Berkeley: Parallax Press, 1991), p. 83.
5. Luke 14:36. *New Oxford Annotated Bible* (Oxford: Oxford University Press, 1977).
6. *Dhammapada*, v. 294.
7. *Digha Nikaya, Sigalovada Sutta* (Rangoon, Burma: Burma Pitaka Association, 1984), p. 442.
8. *Dhammapada*, v. 67–68.

CHAPTER TEN: A Lady of the Night
1. Marye Lilley, ed., *Apadana, Patacara* Part 2 (London: Pali Text Society, 1927), pp. 557–60.
2. Maurice Walshe, trans., *Cakkavathi Sihanada Sutta*, p. 395, and *Kutadanta Sutta*, p. 175, in *Digha Nikaya* (Boston: Wisdom Publications, 1995).
3. Robert Chalmers, ed., *Majjhima Nikaya*, vol. 3 (London: Pali Text Society, 1977), p. 296; and Nyanaponika Thera, *Buddhist Dictionary* (Kandy, Sri Lanka: Buddhist Publication Society, 1970), p. 120.
4. *Dhammapada*, v. 24.

CHAPTER ELEVEN: Fidelity and Faith
1. *Dhammapada*, v. 246–47.
2. Dr. Hammalawa Saddhatissa, *Buddhist Ethics* (New York: George Braziller, 1970), pp. 87–112.
3. *Dhammapada*, v. 215.
4. *Dhammapada*, v. 334.

CHAPTER TWELVE: Buddhist Prosperity
1. E. Hardy, ed., *Anathapindika Sutta*, in *Anguttara Nikaya*, vol. 3 (London: Pali Text Society, 1976), p. 45.
2. A. K. Warder, ed., *Anathapindika Sutta*, in *Anguttara Nikaya*, vol. 1 (London: Pali Text Society, 1961), p. 128.
3. E. Hardy, ed., *Vayagapajja Sutta*, in *Anguttara Nikaya*, vol. 4 (London: Pali Text Society, 1958), p. 281.

4. F. L. Woodward, trans. *The Shopkeeper (B) Sutta: The Book of the Gradual Sayings,* in *Anguttara Nikaya,* vol. 1 (London: Pali Text Society, 1979), p. 100.
5. Ibid., *The Shopkeeper (A) Sutta,* pp. 99–100.
6. Maurice Walshe, trans., *Mahaparinibbana Sutta,* in *Digha Nikaya* (Boston: Wisdom Publications, 1987), p. 236.
7. Ibid., *Sigalovada Sutta,* p. 466.
8. U. Thitthila, trans., *The Book of Analysis: Vibhanga* (London: Pali Text Society, 1988), p. 434.
9. *Dhammapada,* v. 172.
10. *Dhammapada,* v. 224.

CHAPTER THIRTEEN: Healing Powers of Chanting

1. Dr. Lily de Silva, *Spolia Zeylanika,* vol. 36: Part I, *Paritta* (Colombo, Sri Lanka: The National Museums of Sri Lanka, 1981), pp. 3–4.
2. Ven. Dr. K. Sri Dhammananda, *What Buddhists Believe,* 3rd ed. (Kuala Lumpur, Malaysia: Buddhist Missionary Society, 1982), p. 205.
3. Thera Piyadassi, *The Book of Protection* (Kandy, Sri Lanka: Buddhist Publication Society, 1975), pp. 11–21.
4. *Dhammapadaatthakatha, Ayuvaddana Kumara,* vol. 2, p. 235.
5. Richard Morris, ed., *Anguttara Nikaya,* vol. 7 (London: Pali Text Society, 1976), p. 172.
6. *Dhammapada,* v. 183.

CHAPTER FOURTEEN: The London Doctor

1. Richard Morris, ed., *Anguttara Nikaya,* vol. 2 (London: Pali Text Society, 1976), p. 70.
2. Paul Reps, *Zen Flesh, Zen Bones* (New York: Doubleday Anchor, 1955), pp. 41–42.
3. Harvey B. Aronson, *Love and Sympathy in Theravada Buddhism* (Delhi: Motilal Banarsdas, 1980), pp. 78–85.
4. Maurice Walshe, trans., *Sigalovada Sutta,* in *Digha Nikaya* (Boston: Wisdom Publications, 1995), pp. 236, 461.

5. Ven. Dr. K. Sri Dhammananda, *Happy Married Life* (Kuala Lumpur, Malaysia: Buddhist Missionary Society, 1986), pp. 10–23.
6. Maurice Walshe, trans., *Sigalovada Sutta,* in *Digha Nikaya* (Boston: Wisdom Publications, 1995), pp. 236, 461.
7. *Dhammapada*, v. 279.
8. *Dhammapada*, v. 50.

CHAPTER FIFTEEN: Children Change Us

1. Bhikkhu Bodhi, trans., *Abhayarajakumara Sutta,* in *Majjhima Nikaya* (Boston: Wisdom Publications, 1995), p. 498.
2. *Sigalovada Sutta,* in *Digha Nikaya* (Rangoon, Burma: Burma Pitaka Association, 1984), p. 436.
3. Richard Morris, ed., *Anguttara Nikaya,* vol. 1 (London: Pali Text Society, 1961), p. 62.

CHAPTER SIXTEEN: The Alcoholic

1. *Sigalovada Sutta,* in *Digha Nikaya* (Rangoon, Burma: Burma Pitaka Association, 1984), p. 435.
2. *Dhammapada*, v. 173.

CHAPTER SEVENTEEN: Painful Consequences

1. Bhikkhu Bodhi, trans., *Ambalattikarahulovada Sutta,* in *Majjhima Nikaya* (Boston: Wisdom Publications, 1995), p. 525.
2. H. T. Francis, trans., *Bhisapuppha Jataka* (392), in *The Jataka,* vol. 3 (Delhi: Motilal Banarsidas, 1994), p. 192.
3. *Dhammapada*, v. 25.

CHAPTER EIGHTEEN: The Sunbather

1. Bhikkhu Bodhi, trans., *Mulapariyaya Sutta* (1) and *Maharahulovada Sutta* (62), in *Majjhima Nikaya* (Boston: Wisdom Publications, 1995), pp. 83, 527.
2. Bhikkhu Nanamoli, trans., *Visuddhimagga* (Singapore: Singapore Buddhist Meditation Center, 1997), ch. 1, p. 55.

3. Eugene W. Burlingame, trans., *Buddhist Legends*: *Dhamma-pada Commentary*, Part 2 (Cambridge, Mass.: Harvard University Press, 1990), pp. 330–34.

4. *Dhammapada*, v. 412.

CHAPTER NINETEEN: Appearances Are Deceiving

1. E. Hardy, ed., *Vassakara Sutta,* in *Anguttara Nikaya,* vol. 4 (London: Pali Text Society, 1958), p. 183.

2. Eugene W. Burlingame, trans., *Buddhist Legends*: *Dhamma-pada Commentary*, Part 2 (Cambridge, Mass.: Harvard University Press, 1990), pp. 284–86.

3. Eugene W. Burlingame, trans., *Buddhist Legends*: *Dhamma-pada Commentary*, Part 3 (Cambridge, Mass.: Harvard University Press, 1990), pp. 189–91.

4. *Dhammapada*, v. 227.

5. *Dhammapada*, v. 228.

CHAPTER TWENTY: The Seven Types of Wealth

1. E. Hardy, ed., *Satta Dhana Sutta,* in *Anguttara Nikaya*, vol. 4 (London: Pali Text Society, 1958), pp. 4–5.

2. *Dhammapada*, v. 204.

ABOUT THE AUTHOR

Bhante Walpola Piyananda is the founder-president and Abbot of Dharma Vijaya Buddhist Vihara in Los Angeles, California. He was born in 1943, in Walpola, a rural village in Sri Lanka. At the age of twelve, Bhante was ordained as a novice monk. He gave up his lay given name and family name, taking the name of his village "Walpola," and was given the Buddhist name Piyananda, meaning "pleasant joy." Upon assuming the name of his village as his new "surname," in accordance with Sri Lankan tradition, he showed that he now belonged not to his biological family, but to his entire village, typically the widest level of organization in a traditional rural society.

Bhante received his full ordination as a monk, or Bhikkhu, in 1970, and after completing his education in Sri Lanka (B.A. Hon. Kaleniya University) and India (M.A. Calcutta University), he came to the United States for further studies in 1976. Bhante received an additional M.A. from Northwestern University in Chicago in 1980, and in 1985 he completed the requirements for his Ph.D. at the University of California, Los Angeles. He also received a Ph.D from the College of Buddhist Studies in Los Angeles in 1997. Bhante Piyananda is president of the Sangha Council of Southern California, and occupies the position of Chief Sangha Nayaka Thera in America. Over time, he has performed numerous services for Southeast Asian refugee groups in the Los Angeles area, and served as Buddhist Chaplain for the 1984 Olympics. He teaches the Dhamma and meditation at Dharma Vijaya Buddhist Vihara, one of the oldest Theravada Buddhist temples in North America.